PORTLAND
ON THE TAKE

To Woody
Thanks for reading
JD Chandler

PORTLAND ON THE TAKE

MID-CENTURY CRIME BOSSES, CIVIC CORRUPTION & FORGOTTEN MURDERS

JD CHANDLER AND JB FISHER

FOREWORD BY PHIL STANFORD

THE
History
PRESS

Published by The History Press
Charleston, SC 29403
www.historypress.net

Front cover: Police Shotgun Squad. *Courtesy of the Portland Police Historical Society.*
Back cover, top: St. Johns Bridge. *Courtesy of the Portland City Archive.*
Back cover, top inset: Utah Wilson's mug shot. *Courtesy of the Washington State Archive.*
Back cover, bottom inset: Neal Jacoby's mug shot. *Courtesy of the Walter Graven Estate.*

First published 2014

Manufactured in the United States

ISBN 978.1.62619.749.7

Library of Congress Control Number: 2014953176

*To Walter Graven, Earl Anderson, Howard Hanson, Frank Springer,
Don Dupay and all those who did their best.*

"The past lies as a nightmare upon the present."
—Thomas Paine

CONTENTS

FOREWORD

It's always a shock to see how interesting Portland history is once you get past the usual pieties and self-serving narratives of the people who ran the show and generally got away with it all. But the truth is that for much of its existence, starting immediately after the Civil War and continuing at least up to the dawn of the present era, the Rose City has been a hotbed of crime and corruption, watered and fertilized—if you'll pardon the overuse of the metaphor—by the payoff system.

Under this time-honored arrangement, if you wanted to operate any sort of illegal business in Portland—gambling, prostitution, narcotics, you name it—all you had to do was pay off the cops, who would, in turn, pass along a proper share of the take to their bosses in city hall. For decades—especially from the 1930s to the '50s, which is the period *Portland on the Take* focuses on in such fascinating detail—it worked like a charm. Of course, this is not to say that all elected or police officials during this time were on the take. Many were either oblivious or, fearing for their livelihoods, chose to look the other way.

As authors JD Chandler and JB Fisher pointedly remind us, there have always been a few good guys—they actually dedicate their book to several police officers "who did their best"—working within the system to achieve justice on a case-by-case basis. Some of the book's best moments, in fact, come from the long-lost files of sheriff's deputy Walter Graven. These are obviously the true heroes in any account of this sort of systemic corruption, and I salute them as well. And from time to time, there have also been a scattering of civic-minded public officials—such as Dorothy McCullough

FOREWORD

Leé, who served as mayor of Portland from 1949 to 1953—who have attempted to do battle with the institutionalized forces of corruption. "Dottie Do-Good," they called her as she got laughed out of office, and the city settled back into its time-honored way of doing business—politicians on the take, mobsters working hand-in-hand with the cops, murders that get covered up because someone owes somebody a big favor. Read it and weep.

PHIL STANFORD

ACKNOWLEDGEMENTS

So many people have helped to rekindle the embers of this long-forgotten story. Without phenomenal help and support from the Walter E. Graven and Earl Anderson families, the fires would have surely gone out. Thanks also to the helpful staff at the Oregon Historical Society, Portland City Archives, Washington State Archives and the Portland Police Museum. Thank you to Howard Hanson for sharing his memories; to Phil Stanford, Michael Munk, Barney Blalock, JD Chandler, Doug Kenck-Crispin, Andy Lindberg, Finn J.D. John, Heather Arndt Anderson and Joe Streckert for keeping Portland's history invigorating; to Gary Snyder for taking the time to clarify things for me; and to my family for being amazing. A special thanks to Detectives Sam and Nellie Haines, without whose help many of these discoveries would never have come to light!

JB FISHER

I've done this writing thing a few times now, and it never fails to amaze me how much support it takes and how much support is available. First, I would like to thank JB Fisher. Without you, JB, this book would have been just another post on the *Slabtown Chronicle*. Your talent as a researcher is matched only by your skill as a writer. It's been fun. Thanks to all those JB named, especially the Haines Detective Agency, and to many more—Gary Flynn, Mary Hammer, Will McKay, Alex Blendl, Gloria Graven, Matthew

ACKNOWLEDGEMENTS

Anderson, Don Dupay, Theresa Kennedy Dupay, Jim Huff, Kaitlyn Bolduc, Mary Hansen and Brian Johnson. Thank you to all my personal friends and supporters, especially Ken Goldstein, Leslie Sands, Shirley Obitz, Valerie Thibeau, Mitch Priestley, Judy Ostrowski, Diane Rubright, Steve Chandler, Jake Warren and too many more to name. And thank you to all of our supporters on Kickstarter.com. You guys are the greatest. We couldn't have done it without you. Tina Buss Weaver, Sylla McClellan, Greg Applegate, anonymous, Joseph P. Cleary, Virginia K. Platten, Barry Fisher, Timothy Brandis, Michael Hefley, Sylla Gips, Jan West, Jamie Fisher, Jay Yoshihara, Heather Arndt Anderson, Barney Athanasius Blalock, Anna Magruder, Bill Hall, Alexander Craghead, Jennie Herriot, David Blatner, Gary Roberts, David M. Strom, Jim Landman, Catherine McClellan, Kami Horton, Ken Goldstein, David Currie and the good folks at Kick Ass Oregon History. And to you, dear reader: thanks for reading.

JD CHANDLER

THE VICE SCANDAL

If I lived [in Portland], *I would suggest that they fly the flag at half mast.*
—*Senator Karl Mundt*

On Thursday, April 19, 1956, most Portlanders were shocked at the headlines in the daily *Oregonian*. A large banner that read, "City, County Control Sought by Gamblers" introduced a series of articles by Wallace Turner and William Lambert that exposed a pervasive underworld and corruption that spread from the streets of downtown to the highest levels of city government. The series of articles won Turner and Lambert a Pulitzer Prize and brought unwelcome national attention to Portland when the Senate Select Committee on Improper Activities in Labor and Management sent its top investigator, Robert Kennedy, to town. He hauled many prominent Portlanders—including police chief James Purcell, district attorney William Langley and ex-Multnomah County sheriff and newly elected mayor Terry Schrunk—back to Washington, D.C., to testify. Schrunk failed a lie detector test when asked whether he had taken bribes. Langley took the Fifth Amendment rather than answer the question. All three top officials were indicted on their return, but only Langley was convicted.

Kennedy's investigation, like Turner and Lambert's articles, depended on one individual more than any other: James B. Elkins. Elkins was a nondescript man with a flamboyant personality and a genius for self-promotion. For nearly twenty years, he had dominated a large enterprise that involved bootleg liquor, gambling, prostitution and drugs. Using payoffs, blackmail and violence, Elkins, an ex-convict and heroin addict from Arizona, quickly dominated the slot machine/jukebox/pinball industry and then turned it into a highly organized criminal enterprise. Elkins liked to dramatize himself: summoning reporters to midnight meetings, making dramatic threats, wearing a lead-weighted glove for beatings and dubbing himself "Vice Czar." A notorious liar, Elkins convinced Robert Kennedy and his brother John, then a senator and member of the Select Committee, that he told the truth by telling most of it. Elkins was protecting his operation from an attempt by the Teamsters' Union to take it over. The Teamsters, under the leadership of Seattle's Dave Beck, had arguably become a criminal enterprise of its own and was looking to expand into the wide-open town of Portland. In the process, Elkins exposed his own operation, and he never completely recovered.

The story has been told before, best in Phil Stanford's *Portland Confidential* and Robert C. Donnelly's *Dark Rose*. Both books leave important questions unanswered, though. For example: How did Jim Elkins gain so much power? How far did that power really extend? And how did the Teamsters' Union go from being a labor union to a criminal enterprise? It all started with a strike known in Portland as the Big Strike.

1

ALL WE WANT IS A FAIR SHAKE

Our Motto:
An injury to one is an injury to all.
—*International Longshore and Warehouse Union, Local 8*

The year 1934 was one of violent radical change all over the world. Adolf Hitler, elected chancellor of Germany the previous year, seized dictatorial control of his country. As in many European countries that year, revolutionary movements and riots that killed dozens rocked France. In the United States, the newly passed National Recovery Act gave a federal guarantee of the right to organize a union, sparking union organizing drives and violent strikes all over the country. The Teamsters' strike in Minneapolis; the Autolite strike in Toledo, Ohio; and the West Coast waterfront strike challenged the capitalist system and made many feel that the country was on the brink of a revolution.

The 1934 Waterfront Strike, known to a generation as the Big Strike, was like nothing Portland had ever seen. Maritime commerce on the West Coast was shut down for eighty-two days. Lumber and grain exports stopped, and more than fifty thousand Oregon workers lost their jobs, as many as fifteen thousand of them in Portland. There had been strikes, even violent ones, but the Big Strike was a watershed, changing the relationship between workers and employers and leaving its marks on the city for decades to come. Portland already had more than eighty years of history with labor unions since the Brotherhood of Typographical Workers and Printers had organized in 1853. Longshore workers, who loaded and unloaded ships in the Port of Portland,

Union organizers began preparing for the Big Strike years before it occurred. Their work—building solidarity between the waterfront workers and the community at large—was vital in making the '34 strike successful for the International Longshore and Warehouse Union. Photographer unknown. *Courtesy of the Library of Congress.*

were the second group of workers to organize a union in 1868. By the 1930s, many of the city's artisans, professionals and business owner-operators had organized into craft unions; most of these were affiliated with the American Federation of Labor (AF of L).

Craft unions were small, exclusive unions that organized skilled workers into specific job classifications. Craft unions were often run autocratically and served their members by providing group benefits and reducing competition. Most of the craft unions affiliated with the AF of L were independent and rarely coordinated their actions. Employers were often able to pit craft unions against one another in order to weaken the unions' bargaining power and break strikes. The American labor movement owes a great deal to craft unionism for its roots, but shortsighted racist and sexist policies limited the effectiveness of these unions.

The alternative to craft unionism was industrial unionism, exemplified by the Industrial Workers of the World (IWW). The IWW used an inclusive, democratic model of organizing that relied on solidarity across race, gender and class lines. The IWW organized unskilled and unemployed workers for the most part, building class consciousness and mass movements that could put intense pressure on targeted industries. Wobblies, as IWW members were called, used cultural resistance to challenge power, relying on songs, cartoons and jokes to get their points across. For example, one IWW organizer would wait for an opportune moment and then yell, "Help, I'm being robbed." When concerned co-workers would ask what he meant, he replied, "I'm being robbed by the capitalist system." The effectiveness of Wobbly methods and techniques made them a serious threat to the power of employers. Their romantic rhetoric of revolution and commitment to militant confrontation made them easy targets.

Before the Great War, the IWW had made huge strides in organizing loggers and millworkers in the lumber industry, Oregon's largest employer. During the war, a concerted effort between large employers and the United States government used unconstitutional "Anti-Syndicalism Laws" to persecute and destroy the Wobblies and their organization. The Loyal Legion of Loggers and Lumbermen, controlled by the United States War Department, replaced the IWW in the woods and the mills. By 1920, most IWW locals had been shut down, their leaders in jail or killed. Many of the surviving Wobblies drifted into maritime trades, becoming sailors and longshoremen, and found homes in the old waterfront craft unions such as the Sailors' Union of the Pacific (SUP) and the International Longshoremen's Association (ILA). The Wobbly spirit and commitment to industrial unionism was alive in the rank and file membership of the maritime unions, especially in humor and song, but the leadership and the structure of the locals remained firmly in the tradition of craft unionism.

In 1922, a waterfront strike closed the Port of Portland and saw violent clashes between strikers and city police. The employers, represented by the Waterfront Employers' Association (WEA), successfully exploited the contradiction between the industrially minded union members and the limited nature of their craft unions. Support from the Portland police allowed the employers to bring strikebreakers across picket lines and reopen the port. The autonomous nature of the AF of L locals allowed the WEA to pit port against port, weakening the unions' bargaining position and breaking the strike. Like the IWW before it, the ILA was destroyed. On the West Coast, only the tenacious ILA local in Tacoma, Washington, managed to survive.

With the ILA gone, employers were able to control hiring through company-controlled "yellow dog" unions. Yellow dog unions enforced a blacklist that made it impossible for vocal union supporters to get work, forcing them to stay quiet if they wanted to eat. Hiring for longshore jobs was done through the "Shape Up." Eligible longshoremen would show up at the hiring hall, referred to as Fink Hall, in the morning if they were available for work. Dispatchers, often paid for and chosen by the employers, decided who was included in the day's work crews. The dispatcher wielded great power and often demanded bribes and kickbacks in return for work assignments. Pitting worker against worker, the employers reduced wages from ninety-five cents an hour to seventy-five cents and instituted the "Speed Up." The Speed Up demanded fast-paced work and long hours. In the mid-1920s, it was common for longshore work crews to work thirty-six-hour shifts. The workers were afraid to take breaks for fear of blacklisting. Loan sharks

By 1932, there were more than 25,000 unemployed workers in Portland, and 100,000 depended on relief money. Thousands of homeless people lived in Hooverville shantytowns on the east side. Photo by Arthur Rothstein. *Courtesy of the Library of Congress.*

thrived on the waterfront, feeding on the schools of impoverished workers who survived pay envelope to pay envelope. The hiring halls also attracted a criminal element—mostly pimps, burglars and strong-arm thieves—who needed a "visible means of support." They would hang around the hiring halls, gambling and drinking, so they could claim to be longshoremen if they were arrested.

Falling wages, harsh working conditions and unreasonably long hours set the stage for a new organizing drive by the ILA in the late 1920s. In 1929, two organizers set out from Tacoma and visited all of the ports on the West Coast. By 1933, every port had a new ILA local. Although the reborn ILA was still affiliated with the AF of L and based on the craft union model, organizers had learned the lessons of 1922 and did their best to correct earlier mistakes. The ILA was committed to one contract for all the ports on the coast and union control of the hiring halls. It also laid the groundwork for community-wide solidarity by organizing in conjunction with other unions, including the Unemployed Council and student groups on campus at Reed and other colleges. The strong links to the community would be the most important asset that the longshore workers had when it came to a confrontation with their employers.

Falling lumber prices and failing banks brought hard economic times to Portland by 1927. The stock market crash in 1929 brought the Depression in full force. By 1932, when Franklin D. Roosevelt made a campaign stop in Portland, there were more than 25,000 unemployed workers and 100,000 on relief pay. Thousands lived in jerry-rigged housing in "Hooverville" shanty towns that sprang up on the east side of the Willamette. Longshore and sailor jobs were the usual work of last resort for the unemployed. So the rising number of unemployed increased the competition for those jobs. With 1,700 longshoremen dispatched daily on the waterfront, about 1,200 of them were members of ILA Local 38–78. The growing popularity of the union and potential for a strike forced the WEA to raise wages to eighty-five cents per hour in 1932.

Sociologist William Pilcher, in his classic study on Portland longshoremen, shows that by 1934 both the employers and the unions were eager for a strike. The employers were still confident from their win in 1922 and a decade of unchallenged rule on the waterfront. Mayor Joseph Carson had a strict pro-business, anti-union policy, and employers felt sure that he would provide police protection for strikebreakers, just as Mayor George Baker had done in 1922. High unemployment would ease the recruitment of strikebreakers, and if they could be deployed across the hostile picket lines, the strike would suffer the same outcome as a dozen years before. The unions felt ready for the confrontation. With the passage of the National Recovery Act, they would have federal recognition for the first time, and they felt it was time to make the employers recognize them as well. The Unemployed Council (UC), under the leadership of Dirk DeJonge and others, was well organized, and an agreement between the UC and the ILA provided strike funds and donated food to striking longshoremen and the unemployed alike. According to Matt Meehan, business agent of ILA Local 38–78, not one member of the UC crossed the picket lines, and its membership swelled the ranks of the picketers. "During the strike there wasn't one of those unemployed groups, not one man, that scabbed—worked during the strike," said Meehan. "One day there was 5,000 down there on the picket line."

Historians William Bigelow and Norman Diamond explain how unemployed councils sprung up in cities all across the country during the winter of 1929–30. Led by organizers from the Communist Party USA, the councils educated their members on political theory and tactics and took direct action to support their members. In Portland, like most cities, the UC was organized by district; each neighborhood had an elected council. The district council would provide direct action support for the membership in its neighborhood. For example, if a UC member's water was cut off for non-payment of the bill, the UC would send out a team and turn the water back on. The connection between the UC and the ILA was vital for the success of the strike because it made the recruiting of strikebreakers much more difficult and made the large picket lines very effective in shutting down freight terminals.

Months before the waterfront strike began, propaganda squads from the ILA fanned out over Portland's neighborhoods, making contact with working people and small business owners, talking about the issues important to the waterfront workers and making the case for their strike. Propaganda squads continued their activity during the strike, building community solidarity and providing valuable information for the union's nightly "strike update" radiobroadcasts on station KWJJ. The ILA's position was that "scabbing"—working during a strike—was the worst form of theft, taking the food out of the mouths of working families. The police wouldn't stop the theft and often guarded the thieves, so the union had to stop it. The union organized picket squads that kept the union presence visible and established the picket lines. Unions also established flying squads (later disparagingly referred to as "goon squads")—often made up of ex-boxers, wrestlers and football players armed with heavy sticks—to be deployed wherever attempts were made to bring strikebreakers across picket lines. There were even a few unofficial "education committees" that attacked strikebreakers at the hiring halls and, sometimes, in the community at large. Severe beatings were supposed to teach the scabs the seriousness of what they were doing.

In November 1933, the ILA demanded recognition from waterfront employers in all ports on the West Coast. The employers refused. In March 1934, ILA locals in every port on the Pacific coast voted to strike over the issue of union recognition. President Roosevelt personally asked the union to delay the strike, which didn't begin until May 9. The first day of the strike was quiet in Portland. Not much freight was moved, and picket lines were established at every freight terminal. Support from the Sailors' Union, the Teamsters and other maritime unions shut shipping down on the Columbia River. The first confrontation came the next day at Fink Hall at Northwest Ninth Avenue and Everett Street.

The Waterfront Employers Association had set a deadline for 8:00 a.m. on the tenth. Anyone who hadn't shown up for work by that time was fired. It ran a big advertisement reminding the strikers that many of them had lost their homes after the 1922 strike and announcing that at 9:00 a.m. on the tenth, five hundred new jobs as longshoremen would be available in Portland. It was determined to keep the port open. The ILA was just as determined to keep it closed. At 8:00 a.m., 150 work gang bosses showed up at the hiring hall. Working for the employers, they found 100 men willing to break the strike and go to work that day. Outside the building were 1,000 picketers of the ILA and their allies in the Unemployed Council. Sociologist William Pilcher describes the importance of fighting with fists among longshore workers. It is seen as a manly duty to fight for one's rights or for what one believes in. The rhetoric of the Popular Front, which was common among UC organizers such as Dirk DeJonge, portrayed the proletarian as the vanguard of the people's liberation, fighting with his fists for human rights and dignity. The combination of the two led to pugnacious crowds in which fistfights broke out sporadically.

Two buses were parked next to Fink Hall to take strikebreakers to the terminals, but when a few workers tried to board, they were beaten off with fists, and no one got aboard. All morning, 250 men were confined to the hiring hall; the police had to threaten the crowd with tear gas guns in order to bring in lunch for the trapped men. Some of the scabs were able to slip out of the building and disappear into the crowd, but there were still more than 200 men in the hall when the Black Maria paddy wagons from the Central Precinct arrived and started taking strikebreakers out of the building 10 at a time. The crowd of picketers had dwindled to between 300 and 400 by then, and the strikebreakers were able to get away with only a few injuries. Police lieutenant William Epps received a black eye in a scuffle, and several strikers were arrested.

Similar incidents occurred at McCormick Dock and Terminal 1, as well as anywhere else that anyone tried to load or unload anything from ships in Portland. The entire West Coast was shut down with no freight moving and violence in most cities. Matt Meehan, organizer of the ILA, along with more than a dozen other strikers, was arrested on May 10. Police chief Burton Lawson complained that his force was not large enough to keep order, and the city council voted to spend $1,000 to expand the police force with one hundred special officers. Lawson, whose popularity as police chief was destroyed by the strike, complained repeatedly about his force being too small. A more serious problem for him, though, was that many of the officers

Police shotgun squads were used to guard the work crews dispatched from the strikebreaking Columbia River Longshore Association hiring hall in Northeast Portland during and after the 1934 Waterfront Strike. Photographer unknown. *Courtesy of the Portland Police Historical Society.*

supported the strikers and their goals and gave the strikers clandestine aid and intelligence.

The relationship between the strikers and the police was complicated. Officially, the role of the police bureau was to keep order; unofficially, that meant support for the employers opening the port for business. Police chief Lawson and his boss, Mayor Carson, both held anti-union beliefs. But popular support for the striking longshoremen made action on their part politically difficult. The officers of the police bureau were heavily underpaid, and the low level of staffing meant long hours. Throughout the 1930s, twelve-hour shifts were normal, and any emergency was enough to stop days off. Many police officers understood the strikers' grievances and were already beginning to talk about unionizing the force, an event that would happen less than a decade later.

Violent events occurred every day during the strike as the ILA kept the picket lines tight and fought off every attempt the employers made to bring in strikebreakers. On May 14, the Riverboatmen's Union of the Columbia River joined the strike, and it became clear to the employers that they would not be getting the same support from the city that they had come to expect. Frustrated, Mayor Carson pleaded with Governor Julius Meier to send in the National Guard to reopen the port. The next day, the Central Labor Council (CLC) voted for a general strike—shutting down every industry in the city—if the National Guard were deployed. Even worse for the governor, the CLC voted to boycott Meier's family business, the Meier & Frank Department Store, as a warning.

Meanwhile, the ILA showed solidarity with the National Farmers' Union (which had grown to nearly one thousand members in Washington County) by unloading a delivery of sugar that was needed to preserve the fruit harvest. Many farmers would have been ruined for the year if they had not been able to sell their crops to canneries that summer. Things were looking good for the ILA when the union's national leader, Joseph Ryan, flew to San Francisco to negotiate an end to the strike.

The success of the union and its growing power sent chills of fear through the members of the Waterfront Employers' Association. The rising militancy of the working class threatened their power at its base and gave them frightening visions of revolution. Mayor Carson, in his plea to Governor Meier, warned that the city was on the "brink of revolution." Julius Meier, a progressive governor elected on a reform platform, felt his hands were tied, and his response was to delay and call for peace. He warned President Franklin Roosevelt that the situation could result in "open insurrection" if not handled carefully. WEA felt that a quick victory for the union would threaten its power so much that any means of defense was warranted. The employers stonewalled Ryan by refusing to negotiate for the West Coast under one agreement. Instead, they insisted on individual working agreements for each port. Secretly, they began to stockpile supplies and weapons at Terminal 4 in St. Johns, the far north end of Portland.

Members of the WEA also formed the Citizens' Emergency Committee, which would work quietly through the Portland Chamber of Commerce to create an army of "special police"—armed, deputized men—to protect strikebreakers. The "special police" system had been used for nearly one hundred years in Portland and had always been controversial. The specials were deputized with police power but were paid by the employers on their beat. The pay-for-service methods that Portland had always used to compensate its police led to a force that routinely took bribes from businesses that wanted to operate illegally. Police graft was not as systematized and efficient as it would become in the 1940s, but by the '30s, it was completely ingrained in the department and the attitudes of many officers. In 1934, funded by the chamber of commerce, the city hired more than five hundred special officers who worked directly for the Citizens' Emergency League and were led by Major General Ulysses G. McAlexander of the Oregon National Guard and chief of police Burton K. Lawson. The role of the chamber of commerce in the activities of the CEC and CEL was a very closely guarded secret for decades. More than forty years later, historian E. Kimbark MacColl only hinted at it. It wasn't until Michael Munk published his groundbreaking article on the subject in 2000 that the record was exposed. The CEC quickly raised over $100,000 to recruit and arm special police. In the most important break in union ranks, the Portland local of the International Brotherhood of Teamsters contributed to the CEC fund.

Standards for the special police were low, and many of the men hired by the CEL had criminal records or were known to have dangerous tempers. The growing number of special officers included many of the "hall men"—criminals who hung around the hiring hall in order to establish a visible means of support. According to William Pilcher, fighting with fists, sticks and rocks was seen as manly by the longshoremen, but using guns was considered a cowardly act. The special police and strikebreakers had no such compunctions, and all of the shootings that occurred during the strike were cases of specials or strikebreakers firing on unarmed strikers. There were several big fights, including one at McCormick Dock in which nearly two hundred strikers invaded the ship *Admiral Evans*, used for housing strikebreakers and special police, and ran several hundred strikebreakers out of town. One raid on the Nicolai-Neppach mill on Northwest Davis Street confiscated hundreds of heavy clubs that were being made for special police.

The CEC and the Citizens' Emergency League used psychological warfare techniques, including raids on National Maritime Workers' Union (NMWU) picketers disguised as ILA members, as a way to force a split between the ILA and its communist-led allies. The NMWU, the Unemployed Council (UC) and the Young Communist League (YCL) became targets of the police's Red Squad and vigilante raids. Their offices were wrecked and hundreds of their members arrested. Dirk DeJonge, UC organizer and former mayoral candidate, and several others were charged with violating Oregon's Anti-Syndicalism law. DeJonge's attorney was Irvin Goodman, who had made a reputation as champion of the underdog and, over the next twenty-five years, would become the city's leading radical attorney and opponent of the death penalty. Goodman fought DeJonge's conviction all the way to the United States Supreme Court, which finally ruled that the law was unconstitutional. The official attempts to split labor union members from Communists would end up being the biggest legacy of the strike. It brought on a statewide Red Scare that foreshadowed McCarthyism and drastically changed the face of labor unionism in Portland, especially in the waterfront unions.

Longshore picketers, joined by members of the Unemployed Council, blocked railroad lines in Pier Park to keep strikebreakers from entering the freight terminals. Violence often flared during these confrontations. Photographer unknown. *Courtesy of the Portland City Archive A2004-002.9377.*

By the Fourth of July, the employers' preparations were ready. More than five hundred special police had been hired and hundreds of strikebreakers recruited. They were based at the heavily fortified Terminal 4 in St. Johns, which was referred to as "Fort Carson." Joseph Ryan, the national leader of the ILA, made two separate agreements with the employers. Both agreements were voted down by the membership because they allowed the employers to control hiring. Ryan returned to the East Coast in frustration, and the employers prepared for a violent showdown. "Bloody Thursday" on July 5 saw two strikers killed by police gunfire in San Francisco, as well as a successful attempt to regain control of the Seattle port. San Francisco and Oakland responded to the violence with general strikes. The San Francisco General Strike lasted for more than a week, but the strike in Oakland devolved into looting, violence and martial law after only a couple of days. In Portland, a week of fighting climaxed on "Bloody Wednesday" (July 11) when four strikers were shot by a force of specials under the direct command of Chief Lawson. One strikebreaker was accidentally killed in the confrontation near Terminal 4. The political reaction was swift as the CLC prepared for a general strike; the city council voted to fire Chief Lawson, and when Mayor Carson refused, a recall petition for the mayor began to circulate.

Portland avoided a general strike, but days of violence and fighting ensued. Governor Meier wrote frantically to the president asking for federal troops because Portland was in a "state of armed insurrection that could lead to civil war." His letter to Roosevelt ignored the fact that the only shots fired so far had come from the guns of the special police. President Roosevelt, who planned to visit the city in August to dedicate the Bonneville Dam, under construction on the Columbia River, sent New York senator Robert Wagner as his personal envoy to investigate the situation in Portland. In one of the most notorious incidents of the strike, special officers fired on Wagner's car. No one was hurt in the shooting, but several special officers were indicted, and the scandal exposed the trigger-happy private army that the WEA had assembled. The second shooting in less than a week turned public opinion against the employers once and for all. Days later, the WEA agreed to submit the disagreement to federal arbitration, tacitly recognizing the ILA. Within days, the strike was over, and the union was victorious.

Violence didn't stop with the end of the strike, though. Rivalries among the ILA and Teamsters, Sailors' Union of the Pacific (SUP) and the NMWU and ILA strikers and the Columbia River Longshoremens' Association (CRLA) flared into violence several times in August 1934.

The CRLA was a group of longshoremen who broke away from the ILA during the strike and returned to work. They set up their own hiring hall at Northeast Fourteenth Avenue and Alberta Street, referred to by ILA members as "Scab Hall." It would become the scene of the worst violence of the strike. The strike officially ended with a "closed shop" agreement (in which all longshore workers were required to join the ILA) on July 31, but the CRLA continued to dispatch work crews in violation of that agreement. On August 20, nearly one hundred ILA picketers surrounded the converted garage on Northeast Alberta Street, determined that no more work crews would be dispatched. During a violent siege, picketers pelted the building with rocks, several shots were fired and a young strikebreaker from Corvallis, James Conner, was killed and another scab wounded. Marvin Ricks, who was present that day, told historian Michael Munk that an agent provocateur for the police bureau's Red Squad, Harper Knowles, was in the building during the confrontation and probably fired the shots.

Conner's death was used as a weapon against the union; more than thirty union leaders and activists were arrested and charged with murder. The murder case dragged on for years, with most of the union leaders—including Ricks, William O. Fischer and Art Shearer—spending months in jail before the charges were finally dropped against most defendants in May 1935. Juries refused to convict the unionists of a crime since it was clear that they had not had guns and that the shots came from inside the building. Three men were convicted of rioting, and their appeals went on for years.

The main legacy of the strike was a rising militancy among union supporters who learned that city officials would side with employers even at the cost of their political careers. Police chief Burton Lawson was replaced by Captain Harry Niles before the end of the year. The recall petition against Mayor Carson failed to get on the ballot, and he was reelected in 1936. Another major effect of the strike was the split between the unions and the "Communists." The Red Scare that followed the strike encouraged union locals to take drastic action to rid themselves of leftists as labor racketeers and gangsters seized control of more than one of the old AF of L unions. The split in the ILA was not repairable, and the AF of L union was replaced on the West Coast by the more radical Congress on Industrial Organizing (CIO) and the International Longshoremen's and Warehousemen's Union (ILWU) in 1937.

2

RULE OR RUIN:
BEER WARS AND BEYOND

This is terrorism. It is the sort of thing one might look for in gang-ridden Chicago, but not in Portland.
—Oregonian, *July 5, 1935.*

The Big Strike left Portland and other West Coast cities polarized and angry. Employers and workers were more willing to use violence to further their ends. The new governor, Charles Martin, a retired military officer and anti–New Deal Democrat, pursued an openly anti-union policy that was supported by local politicians, such as Mayor Joseph Carson, and the press, such as the *Oregonian.* He explained the increasingly violent conflict as a simple story of unions victimizing employers, businesses and ordinary Portlanders. This oversimplification was far from the truth. Economist H.M. Gitelman and others have convincingly demonstrated that much of the violence in early to mid-twentieth-century America stemmed from the aggressive strategies used by employers, replacing striking workers and deploying armed men to contain and combat them. Another factor that contributed to the violence was competition for contracts or turf between AF of L craft unions and the more radical industrial unions of the CIO. This conflict was often augmented by the insistence of union-affiliated companies that their employees join one or the other of these unions. The violence was also intensified by Governor Martin's anti-Communist rhetoric and the tactics of the Portland Police Bureau's Red Squad, which included infiltration of unions by agents provocateur and propaganda designed to sow distrust and animosity

After the Big Strike of 1934, Portland was a polarized town. Employers and workers were willing to use violent methods to further their ends. Photographer unknown. *Courtesy of the Portland City Archive A2010-001.179.*

among unions. Nowhere is this better illustrated in Portland than in the infamous "Beer Wars" of 1935.

The Beer Wars centered on a dispute between the AF of L's International Brotherhood of Teamsters (IBT) and the Brewery Union Local 320 over jurisdiction in breweries owned by the Northwest Brewing Company (NWBC). Peter Marinoff, president of the NWBC, owned successful breweries in Tacoma and Walla Walla, Washington. In 1934, Marinoff bought Gambrinus Brewery and began selling Marinoff's Red Label Beer in Portland. Workers in Marinoff's Washington breweries were represented by the Brewery Union, but the Teamsters' Union claimed jurisdiction over truck drivers and warehouse workers who distributed the beer. The dispute led to work stoppages and several violent incidents that eventually forced the NWBC out of business.

The Beer Wars made the front page of the *Oregonian* on May Day 1935 after a violent confrontation between Brewery Union truck drivers and Teamsters on the previous day. It wouldn't be long before there was more violence. On

May Day, as the newspaper trumpeted the attack on them from the day before, Oscar Nieman and Ernest Pio, members of the Brewery Union, loaded their truck with Red Label Beer at the Portland distribution center and headed for Vancouver, Washington, to deliver it. As they reached the intersection of Northeast Morgan Street and Union Avenue (today Martin Luther King Jr. Boulevard), a large sedan swerved directly toward them, followed by two other similar vehicles in tight formation. Forced up against the curb by the three cars, the beer truck came to a screeching halt, and Neiman and Pio immediately locked their doors. Trailing behind them and witnessing the ordeal were special police officers John Steik and Don J. Wheeler, employed by the Northwest Brewery Company. The two specials parked their vehicle on the other side of the intersection and headed toward the pinned beer truck. Within moments, no fewer than fifteen men emerged from the three sedans. Brandishing blackjacks, billy clubs and tire irons, they gave Steik and Wheeler no opportunity for conversation. The special officers were beaten senseless and left unconscious on the street. With that, the fifteen men jumped back into the three sedans and sped off. Later that day, John Krieger and a fellow Teamster following an NWBC delivery truck were attacked by three men in another car near the corner of North Vancouver Avenue and Portland Boulevard (now Rosa Parks Way). Krieger received a knife wound on his head in what the *Oregonian* described as a "free-for-all fight." War had begun.

The Great Depression gave the Communist Party excellent opportunities to organize in Portland. The Red Scare that followed the 1934 Waterfront Strike brought intense hostility against Communists. This photo of a 1935 Communist rally is from the Red Squad surveillance files. Photographer unknown. *Courtesy of the Portland City Archive A2001-074.80.*

There was a lull in the violence for several days after the May Day fighting, but both sides engaged in propaganda. Al E. Rosser, secretary of the Teamster truck driver Local 162, asserted in the *Oregonian* that Marinoff had "deliberately violated Teamsters' union contracts." He also called attention to a 1933 AF of L mandate that gave the Teamsters jurisdiction over drivers employed in the brewing industry and the Brewers' Union jurisdiction over workers inside the plants, a classic craft union structure. Rosser implied that Marinoff's allowing Brewery Union members to drive delivery trucks was responsible for the violence. Marinoff countered the charges with large advertisements in the *Oregonian* stating that the company was "fair to ALL organized labor."

The brief calm was shattered after Jack Schlacht, James Scott and Jack Estabrook, all members of the Teamsters' Union, were indicted for the beating of Steik and Wheeler on May 14. All three men pleaded "not guilty," and violence resumed almost immediately. The situation escalated significantly when William Usitalo, a Teamster, was shot to death while picketing Marinoff's Tacoma brewery. Five armed guards employed by Marinoff were held as Usitalo's killers. Among them were thugs and disgraced police officers of "notoriously bad character." Marinoff himself was arrested and charged with manslaughter, although the charges were eventually dropped. One special officer was convicted of assault, and the case disappeared from the newspapers.

From late May into July 1935, bricks were repeatedly hurled from

MARINOFF
is fair to
ALL ORGANIZED
LABOR

INTERNATIONAL UNION
UNION MADE
AFFID... a FofL
OF U.B.F.C. & S.D.W.
OF AMERICA

Marinoff Beer is made and delivered by United Brewery Workers of America

ASK FOR AND DEMAND RED LABEL BEER

Peter Marinoff tried to show his support for unionism with this ad, but it didn't help in his conflict with the Teamsters' Union. *Courtesy of BreweryGems.com.*

speeding sedans into numerous beer parlors around Portland, and at least four bombings were reported. These included the May 30 blast at Bill Fuegy's Rock Creek store (today McMenamin's Rock Creek Tavern), which left a small crater outside the building, and a "time bomb" at the Madison Square Garden beer parlor toward the end of June that spurred Portland police captain John J. Keegan to order his men "to shoot to kill" to quell "these gangster tactics." While many Portlanders were quick to blame unionists for the attacks, both the brewery union and the Teamsters publicly offered fifty-dollar rewards for help in "running down outside vandals" apparently responsible for the bombings and brick throwing. Despite such gestures, however, evidence pointed in the direction of union members themselves.

When Barnacle Bill's beer parlor on Northeast Broadway was severely damaged by a black powder bomb just before Independence Day, for instance, the establishment's owner, W.H. Dillshaw, related to detectives how, during the previous week, "two men, one tall and one short, had been in his place and demanded that he change the brand of beer offered for sale." Versions of this story were reported following brick hurling incidents at the Blue Baboon Café on Southwest Fourteenth Avenue and Jefferson Street, at the El Trojan Café on North Williams Avenue, at Wimpy's at 1138 Northwest Twenty-first Avenue and at other vandalized beer parlors. This evidence was convincing to many, but the role of the police bureau's "Red Squad" complicated the picture.

The Red Squad was founded in 1919 as part of the campaign against the Industrial Workers of the World (IWW). Walter B.

Walter Odale of the Portland Police Bureau used the Red Squad as not only an intelligence gathering body but also a weapon of propaganda. Using smear campaigns and agents provocateur, Odale encouraged the violence that marked the labor movement in Portland in the 1930s. Photographer unknown. *Courtesy of the Portland Police Historical Society.*

Odale, a Portland policeman since 1910, took a five-year leave of absence from the force to serve in the army during the Great War. In 1922, he returned to Portland and took over the nascent Red Squad. The mission of the squad was to "combat radical activity," and Odale took it seriously. He also took it to great extremes, releasing lists of names of people he said were Communists, interfering in elections by making unsubstantiated accusations against candidates and infiltrating organizations of all types with agents provocateur and informants. The activities of the Red Squad and its successor, the Intelligence Division, were veiled in secrecy. Every mayor from George Baker to Vera Katz denied its existence, and details have come out only through investigation by journalists and historians, such as Phil Stanford and Michael Munk.

Although the Red Squad was partially funded by the city, the majority of its funding came from private citizens and groups such as the American Legion, which cooperated fully with the Red Squad and was sometimes indistinguishable from it. Under the loose control of police captain John Keegan, for much of its life, the Red Squad operated independently from the rest of the police bureau and kept its headquarters outside the police station. The relationship between the Red Squad and the Teamsters' Union was very convoluted. Al Rosser, who rose to be head of the Teamsters' Union in Oregon before being convicted of an arson plot, was closely associated with George Stroup, head of the American Legion's "Americanization Committee" and a hidden member of the Red Squad. At least one of the Teamsters indicted in the city's "war on goons" was reputed to be an agent provocateur for the Red Squad. While the name of the infiltrator was never revealed, the use of agents provocateur by the Red Squad was revealed during the 1939 trial of Harry Bridges, president of the International Longshore and Warehouse Union, when Merriel Bacon of the police bureau admitted infiltrating the Portland Communist Party and acting as an informer and provocateur from 1930 until 1937. Also at that trial, Al Rosser and Jack Estabrook, both of the Teamsters' Union, admitted making regular payments to Captain Keegan "for protection."

John Keegan had a long career with the police bureau, involved with both the Red Squad and the vice squad, and rose to the position of chief of detectives. He took payoffs in all the positions he held and often seemed to be more interested in theater than law enforcement. His big break came on July 12, 1935, when he and his men rounded up nine Teamsters suspected in the Beer War bombings and brick throwing. Triumphantly proclaiming that he had broken up "this gangsterism," Keegan accused the Teamsters of "dragging a red herring across the trail" by offering to aid police and providing rewards to clear up the bombings, "and here they are in the midst of it." Accusations against the Teamsters became even more pointed in late August when Jack Estabrook surrendered to a warrant charging him with assault of the two special officers back in early May. Within several months, Estabrook was acquitted in that case, and the nine Teamsters apprehended for the rash of beer parlor bombings saw their charges dismissed.

In 1938, the Northwest Brewery Company was a distant memory, and Peter Marinoff relocated to California. The Red Squad, now working with the statewide intelligence apparatus set up by Governor Martin, was not through with the Teamsters,

Mayor Joseph Carson participated fully in Governor Martin's red scare using the police bureau's Red Squad to infiltrate and attack organizations such as the American Civil Liberties Union. Photographer unknown. *Courtesy of the Portland City Archive A2004-001.557.*

though. As part of the city's "war on goons," Jack Estabrook, now secretary of the warehouse branch of the Portland Teamsters, was indicted for the 1935 bombing of Bill Fuegy's Rock Creek store. Two accomplices, Melvin Bozarth and Leon V. Wallingford, admitted to the bombing and fingered Estabrook. LeRoy Frank Cooper, the Teamsters' self-proclaimed "powder man" and suspected Red Squad infiltrator, had also come forward to implicate Estabrook. The trial lasted until May 24, 1938, when the jury failed to come to a verdict. The jury in a subsequent retrial also failed, although in the course of that trial, Portland papers revealed how "jurors in the first trial…had been embarrassed by publication of their names and addresses [in the newspapers] through fear of being molested." A third trial featuring a sequestered jury finally found Estabrook guilty of vandalism, and on September 18, 1938, he was sentenced to eighteen months in prison. In addition to the sentence, he was handed a bill for $3,566 (about $56,000 in 2014) from the state to cover the cost of three trials.

Less than a year later, while still awaiting appeal, Estabrook found himself in the clear. During the California trial over the proposed deportation of longshore leader Harry Bridges, the payoffs from the Teamsters to Portland police captain Keegan were exposed. While the extent of the payoffs will never be known with certainty, the explanation given by all parties involved was that the Portland police were protecting Teamster leader Dave Beck against assassination attempts, and Estabrook and Rosser were providing the funds. Revelation of payments between the Teamsters and the Portland police effectively ended the Beer Wars once and for all. However, attention to internecine strife between unions and employers in the news media was on the rise. Rather than reporting on the complex and sometimes shifting battle lines that might pit unions against rival unions (as in the case of the Beer Wars), the press opted to present a simple and clear-cut tale of employers and citizens facing unrelenting picketers who often relied on violent squads of "goons" and "terrorists" to carry out their agendas.

Many labor supporters accused officials of "unduly sensationaliz[ing]" the situation. But this did not quell the efforts against unions by Governor Martin, Mayor Carson and city councilman Earl Riley, and it certainly did not silence the papers. The year 1938 saw a veritable "goon craze" in the Portland news media, culminating with a series of articles authored by Herbert Lundy, called "The Oregon Goons," appearing in the Sunday *Oregonian Magazine* throughout the month of August. With the subtitle "How a Small Number of Men Ignored the Laws and the Community Until Public Opinion Sent them to the Jails and to the Penitentiary," Lundy's stories captured the imagination of Portland readers and reinforced the position that unionists and the business community were always diametrically opposed to each other.

In one of the first stories, "Death Comes to a Young Man," Lundy told a highly slanted tale of the death of James Conner during the 1934 Waterfront Strike. Lundy told how a "young Oregon State College student," James Conner, was shot dead by four ILA members while trying to seek employment on the waterfront during his summer vacation. He claimed that the "ILA fought with every means available to prevent its four members from serving six months in jail for contempt," failing to mention the acquittals or the evidence against the Red Squad.

Subsequent articles described a stream of seemingly senseless violent acts by labor organizers, strikers and "terrorist" thugs against employers, strikebreakers and non-union-affiliated employees. Perhaps most noteworthy of all were the descriptions of the "rule or ruin" tactics employed by Al Rosser, apparently to assert Teamster authority in Portland. Several former associates, testifying under indictment, described Rosser's indiscriminately reckless tactics. Teamster William E. Martin, for example, explained it this way:

> [W]*e told Al Rosser about a gas tanker that was hauling Richfield gasoline from the plant at Linnton to a reserve tank on Columbia Slough…and that transports were picking up gas from this reserve tank and hauling it to eastern Oregon. At this time, Rosser said: "Either burn the place or dynamite it, one of the two but be sure to get it." We told him that this would endanger some other property there and that there was a small living quarters north of the tank and he said: "To hell with it. Let it go too."*

It should be noted, however, that neither a fire nor an explosion took place at that particular location.

Several other noteworthy cases centered on the testimony of Alfred Turpin, an AF of L mechanic who had been arrested and held by John

The St. Johns Bridge, opened in June 1931, was allegedly the central focus of a bomb plot during a dispute between AF of L craft unions and the CIO Millworkers' Union. Photographer unknown. *Courtesy of the Portland City Archive A2004-002.955.*

Keegan's Red Squad in January 1938. As Lundy described it in his August 14 "Goons" installment, Turpin aroused the attention of Deputy Sheriff Holger Christofferson and Undersheriff Martin Pratt while pacing his cell and "ranting" about his involvement in the late January bombing of the Dral Cleaning & Dyeing Works in Southeast Portland. In that case, Turpin and others had set off a dynamite explosion on the second floor of the building, badly damaging both the business and its owner's home next door. "Labor difficulties" were identified as the motive, although no specifics were given.

Turpin also related his involvement in several attempts to blow up two boats involved in lumber union disputes in the fall of 1937. Turpin and several AF of L associates targeted the schooner *W.R. Chamberlain* and the tugboat *Lyle H* for their affiliation with the Jones Lumber Company. AF of L pickets against "hot cargo"—cargo loaded by rival union members—got into a rock fight with CIO millworkers loading lumber aboard the *Lyle H* on September 10, 1937. Following a "three week tie-up behind A. F. of L. [*sic*] picket lines," the *Chamberlain* was moved to Astoria, where strikers turned it away.

Arriving back in Portland, both the ship and the tug docked below the St. Johns Bridge in North Portland. The *Chamberlain*'s captain, Luther Jacobsen, had ignored an apparent agreement with strikers to relocate the ship to San Pedro, California. According to Turpin, he and several associates were ordered by fellow unionist Harlow King to "go down and blow that damn *Lyle H* up." The vigilance of the harbor patrol and bright searchlights at the dock prevented direct access, so Turpin, Tony Sunserie and James Duffy parked their vehicle on the St. Johns Bridge. Lundy's article quotes Turpin describing the episode:

> *Tony was sitting in the front seat with me and Duffy was in the rear seat with the bomb. Duffy lit the bomb in the back seat while we were driving. Tony jumped out of the car and Duffy handed him the bomb. Tony was quite a ways from the* Lyle H *and had to run up the bridge quite a ways in order to get to throw the bomb. Tony jumped back in the car after throwing the bomb and we came back to town…I did not hear any explosion after the bomb was dropped over, but the fuse was a 30-minute fuse so that I was pretty near to town before it should have went off* [sic].

The first attempt failed to hit the boat, but the trio tried again the next night (which happened to be Armistice night). This time, Sunserie threw three bombs off of the bridge, but none hit the target. No explosions were reported in St. Johns, so apparently the bombs went into the river without exploding.

Months later, while docked at San Pedro, the *Chamberlain* fell victim to sabotage when another of Turpin's associates succeeded in putting "emery powder" in the propeller shaft. The ship "barely limped into Frisco" after crews worked tirelessly to clean out the debilitating additive. While Lundy's article ended by praising Portland police captain Keegan, prosecutor Ralph Moody and state police captain Vayne Gurdane for their success in obtaining numerous "goon" confessions starting with Turpin's, no additional details were provided regarding the actual union disputes that led to the violence. It is telling, too, that Ralph Moody, Governor Martin's special prosecutor for "goons," did not differentiate between the AF of L and the CIO when prosecuting union men, according to historian Gary Murrell.

Along with sensational tales of dynamite bombs flying from the St. Johns Bridge, Lundy's "Goon" articles also retold the story of the Beer Wars, this time focusing simply on the arrest of "Teamsters Union business agents" for rioting in their attempts to stop "a truck on Union Avenue and engag[e] in a fight." There was no mention that workers from a rival union were driving the truck nor that Northwest Brewing Company and its owner, Peter Marinoff, were proudly affiliated with that same union. And certainly there was no mention of the recently disclosed financial relationship between the Teamsters and the chief "goon" hunter, Portland police captain John Keegan.

In the last installment of Lundy's "Goon" articles, published on Sunday, August 28, 1938, a large chart took up significant real estate on the second page. Titled "Here's How They Stand," the chart divided into three columns the names, pleas and dispositions of dozens of men indicted on "labor terrorism" charges over the previous several years. Further categorized by counties across Northwest Oregon, as well as Skamania County, Washington, the list included many of the key figures discussed above. The St. Johns Bridge bomb plotters each spent eight months in jail, and many of the Teamsters involved in the Beer Wars were, at that point, awaiting trial or sentencing (most were eventually acquitted or served shortened jail time). Of the nearly fifty names listed in the Multnomah County section, none was serving a sentence longer than two years, and most faced six to eight months in jail. Whether the minimal punishments had anything to do with financial collusion between city government and union organizations cannot be known with certainty, but for all the brouhaha coming from the news media, as well as from law enforcement officials and roused citizenry, the so-called terrorist violence that swept Portland in the 1930s did not match the sensationalized hype.

3

THE CRIMINAL ELEMENT

*Organized crime is nothing more than capitalism with the mask of
respectability removed.*
—*Dave Mazza*

Prohibition ended in 1933. In response, bootleggers and other criminals
started looking for new fields to replace the profitable businesses they
had established. Labor racketeering, in which gangsters took over labor
unions and used them as criminal enterprises, became a growth industry.
The volatile labor situation in Portland created lots of opportunities, but
the leadership of the underworld was in transition. Royden H. Enloe, who
controlled the city's slot and vending machines, had been a pioneer in the field
of "labor slugging"—hiring out anti-union "beat up squads"—during the
1922 Waterfront Strike. Bobby Evans, the city's most important bookmaker
and reputed vice lord, had received a great deal of publicity during the Public
Market Scandal of 1932 and had been keeping a low profile ever since.
Personal problems made Enloe vulnerable, and a new generation was ready
to make a bid for power. By the end of the decade, James Elkins had replaced
Enloe, and Al Winter had superseded Evans.

Vice has always been good business in Portland. From the time William S.
Ladd arrived on Front Street in 1851 with a load of wholesale booze, fortune
and power have been built on a foundation of vice. From the earliest times,
saloons in Portland provided gambling and prostitution to go along with
the drinks. One of the city council's first ordinances outlawed gambling;
but the law was never seriously enforced, except against outsiders. By the

1880s, the city's richest and most powerful men were deriving at least some of their income from vice, and the city depended on liquor sales for up to 70 percent of its annual income. James Lappeus, the police chief, owned Portland's swankiest saloon and gambling parlor, and district attorney John Caples owned buildings in the North End that housed prostitutes. In fact, Caples selectively enforced the city's anti-prostitution laws to drive women out of the Tenderloin, located prominently downtown, to the North End, where he happily rented his buildings to them. Caples was an early advocate of the "wide-open" North End, an enduring idea. In 1905, Fred T. Merrill, the Bicycle King of the Northwest, ran for mayor on a platform of keeping the city wide open.

Larry Sullivan, the sailors' boardinghouse master of the 1890s, and Frank Woon, of the Hop Sing Tong in the 1870s, are two of the earliest examples of crime bosses in Portland. Sullivan preyed on sailors and transient workers; Woon, on Chinese people. They both cooperated with the city government and the police; both collected most of their income from liquor, gambling and prostitution; and both used violence to enforce their will and maintain their power. Larry Sullivan didn't last long. Alcoholism and marital problems sent him on a search for greener pastures and a sad end. The organization that Frank Woon created in Portland, the Hop Sing Tong, is still in operation, going on its second century. Its activities have been shrouded in secrecy and its code of silence effectively enforced. Widely reported arrests in the 1990s showed that the organization continued to be involved in illegal activity.

Crime and vice are activities for entrepreneurs in Portland. Anyone with enough capital can open a legitimate business, supplement their income illegally and use the money to buy influence in the community. A wrong step can send them to jail and ruin the plan, but it is a little surprising how often it works. Working people with little capital have the opportunity to acquire it through armed robbery or burglary. A good manager can turn a small crew of earners into a powerful organization. No one in Portland has done that more effectively than James B. Elkins, a petty criminal and grifter who came to Portland in 1937, but it has happened hundreds of times before him and just as many since. After Larry Sullivan's time, the Hop Sing Tong continued to control vice and crime in Chinatown, but the rest of the underworld had no major leader. Small-time operators ran gambling, booze and prostitution joints in the North End and other neighborhoods. The police supplemented their income by looking the other way, being goaded to action from time to time only by outraged public opinion that soon died down. The political

Police chief Leon Jenkins (pictured here second from left) might not have been in on the $100,000 per month payoff, but his force was used to keep down the competition during Prohibition. Photographer unknown. *Courtesy of the Portland Police Historical Society.*

establishment profited from these activities, and everybody but Portlanders thought of Portland as a wide-open town.

Progressive Oregon voted in prohibition in 1914, but the citizens had plenty of time to get used to it. The Dry Law didn't take effect until January 1, 1916, and it came in stages. The state didn't go bone-dry until November 1916, and even then, some alcohol was allowed for personal use. According to Floyd R. Marsh, a member of Portland's vice squad during Prohibition who published his memoirs in 1976, the city was the central point for distribution of Canadian whiskey, and over $100,000 a month was paid out to officials of Multnomah County and the City of Portland. Hundreds of speakeasies and beer or wine parlors were allowed to operate in the city, and the profits were funneled into gambling enterprises and prostitution that flourished around those locations. Business was good, and opportunities to expand into other legitimate and illegitimate businesses abounded. According to Marsh, the Portland police seized liquor from anyone who tried to compete with the city's "approved" bootleggers. The evidence room in the basement of the central pecinct became the liquor cabinet for the mayor and his cronies, and much of it made its way into the hands of established bootleggers. As Dave Mazza, the former editor of the *Portland Alliance*, pointed out, organized crime is nothing more than the ruthless application of capitalist principles, and it is natural for businesses to expand. The lack of a strong leader left a vacuum that some were eager to try and fill.

One of the city's "approved" bootleggers was "Yam" Wallace. He established himself as the underworld king of Black Portland through a network of railroad porters who imported bonded whiskey from Canada. Wallace ran his operation from the Golden West Hotel and reigned over bootlegging, gambling and prostitution in African American clubs with an "iron hand," according to the *Oregonian*. Tom Johnson worked as a distributor for Wallace until the two men had a falling out in 1921. During a confrontation, Johnson drew a knife and cut Wallace severely. From his hospital bed, Wallace threatened Johnson's life but soon was arrested with nearly $10,000 worth of cocaine and sent to prison for the rest of his life. Wallace's timely arrest left the field clear, and Johnson took over his operations. Johnson, born to ex-slaves in Louisiana in 1883, came to Portland by way of Eastern Oregon in 1910. He was rumored to have been part of a ring of armed robbers in California but soon set himself up as owner of the Orpheus Club near the corner of Northwest Fifteenth Avenue and Savier Street. Over the next fifty years, Johnson extended his power and wealth, using Portland's segregated housing policies to his own advantage as he became the largest African American property owner in town.

Regardless of segregation, though, two fields of gambling tended to dominate the vice industry in Portland: slot machines and bookmaking. Both enterprises generated large cash incomes that could be easily skimmed or used for laundering money from other enterprises. Bookmaking, betting on horse races or other sporting events, is as old as sports and usually was run through cigar stores. Schiller's Cigar Store, at the corner of Southwest Fourth Avenue and Washington Street, was the earliest center for sports betting in Portland. W.C. "Jerry" Powers, who worked behind the counter, took bets and posted odds on a huge chalkboard. Powers did big business, taking more than $30,000 worth of bets on the 1907 mayoral election, eventually opening a poolroom in the basement of the Perkins Hotel. Slot machines were invented in San Francisco in 1895 and introduced into Portland the next year. They caught on quickly and became very popular. By 1900, slot machines were located in most saloons, many shops and even shoeshine stands all over Portland.

Portland's first "slot-machine king" was S. Morton Cohn. Slot machines, soon dubbed "one-armed bandits," were invented as gambling devices, and the city began its long campaign to suppress them soon after the turn of the twentieth century. Cohn attempted to take gambling out of the equation, first by introducing slot machines that paid off in cigars and, in 1904, inventing the "coin-in-the-slot" shoeshine machine. For many years, the city considered any coin-operated machine a gambling device and attempted to control it with license fees, ordinances and raids. The machines were legalized piece-meal over many years; lawsuits often had to go to the Supreme Court. Cigar machines were legalized first, jukeboxes in 1930 and pinball machines not until the 1950s. Cohn expanded his business into vaudeville and movie theaters, and by the time of the Great War, he had moved into the more respectable business of real estate development. He left slot machines to his ambitious and ruthless employee Royden H. Enloe.

Royden Enloe soon began buying his coin-operated machines from Al Capone's Chicago outfit and using Capone's brutal methods to expand and protect his business. He recruited squads of ex-boxers, wrestlers and football players to do his strong-arm work, although he was not above a little hands-on action of his own, especially with women. Enloe used brutal strong-arm methods to force shop owners to use his machines and to run his competition out of business. Running a blatantly illegal operation, Enloe needed protection from the police, and he got it from a man with excellent city connections: Augustine C. Ardiss, more popularly known as "Matchmaker" Bobby Evans.

Bobby Evans was a popular prizefighter in the first decade of the twentieth century. Retiring before the Great War, Evans began to manage boxers, and in 1920, he was appointed matchmaker by the Portland Boxing Commission. Evans was accused of crimes many times, from fixed fights to burglary, and he was known as the head of bookmaking in Portland after the murder of Jerry Powers in 1921. Powers was killed in his Perkins' Hotel poolroom during an apparent robbery. His killer, an Austrian, was quickly found, convicted, pardoned and deported. There is no evidence that Powers's murder was anything but a robbery gone bad, but the quick and quiet handling of his murderer and Evans's consolidation of power after his death make it highly suspicious.

Rumors of Evans's connection with the East Coast crime syndicate were persistent. His typical answer when asked about it was: "I don't know what

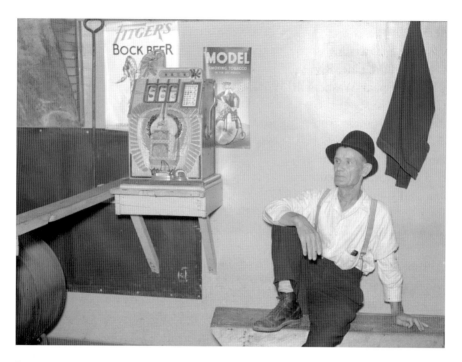

By the 1930s, slot machines were a common sight in taverns, shops and even shoeshine stands. Al Capone's Chicago outfit exported them, along with their violent tactics, to towns and cities all over the west. Photograph by Russell Lee. *Courtesy of the Library of Congress.*

you're talking about." The only proven connection to the Mob was through one of Evans's associates, boxer Mike DePinto, who was arrested in 1952 as part of the narcotics ring run by Waxey Gordon. DePinto, along with his brothers Nick and Ray, ran one of the most violent criminal gangs in Portland history. In alliance with other immigrants living in South Portland, such as Abe Weinstein and Jack Minsky, the DePintos were involved in bootlegging, prostitution, gambling and burglary. By 1932, they were the most powerful criminal gang in the city. In a campaign that involved at least four bombings and an unknown number of deaths, the DePintos attempted to take control of vice in Portland by running their competitors out of town. The overt violence was the end of the DePinto gang, as more than fourteen people were arrested in the plot. The DePintos and many of their accomplices went to jail. The rumor was that Bobby Evans was behind the plot, but he never faced charges over the bombings.

It was not just recent immigrants who were involved with organized crime—pioneer families sometimes had their black sheep as well. Joseph

"Frenchy" LaTourell, a French-Canadian born in New York, came to Oregon on a whaling ship in 1855. He married Grace Ough, daughter of Dr. McLoughlin's aide, Richard Ough, and White Wing of the Chinook people who lived near Washougal, Washington. Frenchy and Grace settled on the Columbia River near Rooster Rock, upstream from Portland. Frenchy ran a tugboat and piloting business, and Grace provided hospitality and nursing at their early version of a roadhouse. Their brood of fifteen children became famous for their musical and dancing abilities. The small lumber mill town that grew around their landing was soon called LaTourell, and the creek and waterfall there still bear the family name. The LaTourell children, who spelled their names in various ways (LaTourelle, LaTarrelle), had many talents and achievements (including the first female mayor of Troutdale, Clara LaTourell Larson), but the family had a black sheep. His name was Lucien "Lover" LaTourelle. He was born in 1900, and he came to Portland at the age of seventeen. He soon caught the eye of the Portland Police Bureau.

The Great War brought prosperity that Portland had not seen since the gold rush of the 1850s and '60s. During the war, Portland, with its vast supply of lumber, became one of the primary shipbuilding ports of the West Coast. Population in the city soared, and the wide-open town provided entertainment of all kinds to shipbuilders, sailors and soldiers. Lola Baldwin of the Police Women's Protective Division went to work for the United States Army and did her best to impose "moral martial law" on the West Coast, but it was a losing battle. In 1917 and 1918, venereal disease rates soared in Portland, and for a while, the United States Navy declared the city "off limits." Crime rates soared, too, as the open vice attracted criminals from other cities, and deserting soldiers and sailors eagerly joined them. Lover LaTourelle was arrested the first time for an armed robbery at a grocery store that he pulled with two AWOL sailors in 1918. He went to jail for a year and, somewhere along the way, picked up a heroin habit. By 1920, the handsome young man, who often dyed his hair as a disguise, specialized in recruiting young women from prominent Oregon families. Working out of a downtown rooming house owned by his sister, LaTourelle held "select parties" that featured the use of cocaine and heroin. Addiction to heroin or cocaine required $100 to $200 per week to obtain the drugs. Desperate young addicts were ripe for seduction into prostitution.

Lucien LaTourelle did not restrict his activities to drugs and prostitution, though. In 1932, Lucien and his wife, Frances, were arrested inside a home on Southeast Hawthorne Boulevard. They were charged with a series of burglaries in east Portland, but before the case could come to trial, Lucien suddenly died. Dr. DeNorval Unthank, Portland's first African American physician, announced LaTourelle's death but did not mention its cause. His timely death kept Lucien out of jail, but his nephew Richard carried his tradition into the next decade. Richard LaTourelle, the son of Lucien's brother Andrew and Clara Larson, grew up at LaTourell Falls. His father died in a boating accident in 1918, and Clara remarried. In 1940, now a widow for the second time, Clara and her son bought the Hotel Clare at 314 West Burnside Street. Located a block from the west end of the Burnside Bridge and across the street from the Sailors' Union of the Pacific office, the Clare was soon known as a "skid road" hotel. The blocks around the hotel contained taverns, brothels and rooming houses, most of which catered to sailors. The first arrests for prostitution were made at the Hotel Clare soon after Richard LaTourelle took over. Burke's Café, directly across the street, soon became an important distribution point in the heroin trade as well.

Matchmaker Bobby Evans met his own Waterloo in 1932, during the scandal over the Seawall Public Market. Allegations of bribery involving Mayor George Baker and several members of the city council spurred a recall movement against Baker, councilmen John Mann and Earl Riley and district attorney Lotus Langley. Evans masterminded the burglary of the campaign office that stole hundreds of recall petitions, most of them for Langley, according to Yvette "Betty" Moore, the main witness against Evans. The burglary was effective. Not enough signatures were collected to recall Langley or Riley. Councilman Mann was recalled and retired from public life. Mayor Baker narrowly survived his recall election and then wisely decided not to run for reelection. In December 1932, Bobby Evans was tried and acquitted on charges of burglary. His acquittal seems to have been a foregone conclusion since Langley supervised the prosecution of his case. Evans continued to be involved in boxing and bookmaking for many years, but he kept a much lower profile after the bad publicity.

Meanwhile, a young lawyer and sports enthusiast, Alfred F. Winter, began to consolidate control of bookmaking after 1932. Winter, the son of Judge John P. Winter, graduated from the Northwest School of Law in 1923 and was admitted to the bar in 1925. Law was never a big interest of his; he was much more interested in the sporting life. By the early 1930s, he was running a club on Southwest Fourth Avenue that featured betting on dart games and other sporting events. After an arrest for running banned dart games, Winter fought in court, and in 1936, dart games were ruled legal. A short time later, Winter opened the Turf Smoke Shop on Southwest Park Avenue, continuing the tradition of cigar stores operating as betting parlors. In 1940, Winter opened the Pago Pago Room in the same building as the Turf Club. The Pago Pago Room became one of the most popular and well-known nightclubs in Portland during and after the Second World War. Winter, a childhood friend of city councilman and later mayor Earl Riley had good relations with the city, and by the end of the '30s, he was considered the leader of organized crime in Portland, collecting tribute from Royden Enloe, the slot machine king, and "Shy Frank" Kodat, who ran a burglary/armed robbery ring on the east side, among others. The Federal Bureau of Investigation (FBI) alleged that Winter was an associate of Louis Dragna, son of Los Angeles mobster Jack Dragna and later head of the Los Angeles crime family, but "Big Al" always denied the charge, saying, "You must be thinking of someone else."

Winter was still consolidating his power in 1937 when James Elkins arrived in Portland. Elkins was a high school dropout born in Texas in 1901 who had a criminal record going back to a vagrancy charge in Salt Lake City when he was nineteen. Rolla Crick, a reporter for the *Oregon Journal* and later the *Oregonian*, traced Elkins's criminal career through a series of charges for car theft, burglary and narcotics smuggling. A 1932 burglary in Nogales, Arizona, in which Elkins fired a pistol at a police officer, brought his longest jail sentence: twenty to thirty years in the Arizona State Penitentiary. Elkins had connections of some kind because he served less than five years. Crick said that he had "bought a pardon," and by the summer of 1937, Elkins

Longtime police officer Harry Niles took over as chief of police after the Big Strike. He was interested in improving the image of the police bureau but had little interest in stopping organized crime or the graft that came with it. Photographer unknown. *Courtesy of the Portland Police Historical Society.*

had resettled in Portland. Elkins's brother, Fred, was already established, running a small brothel and working with a bootlegging gang. Jim Elkins had bigger plans.

Elkins was a notorious liar, dramatizing and embellishing his career. He loved to play on his reputation as a tough guy, and in the 1950s, he liked to refer to himself as Portland's "Vice Czar." During the vice scandal and McClellan Committee hearings in 1956–57, Elkins claimed that he never participated in prostitution or drug dealing, but those were lies in an attempt to cast himself as the "good guy." Jim Elkins was involved in running his brother's brothel, and his main priority on arriving in Portland was to secure a steady supply of opiates to feed his long-term addiction. He recruited a crew of young toughs to assist in his plans. One of his recruits was Harry Huerth, a young burglar and "box man" who specialized in opening safes. Huerth, who published his memoirs in 1972 under the name Harry King, said that Elkins put him on a regular salary and set him to work robbing drugstores. The deal was that Huerth could keep any money he took in his burglaries, as long as he kept Elkins supplied with dope.

With a steady supply of opiates, Elkins was ready to establish himself, and Royden Enloe's slot machine empire was vulnerable. By the 1930s, Enloe's situation had deteriorated. The fall of the DePinto gang and the 1934 Waterfront Strike had resulted in a lot of bad publicity for the administration of Mayor Joseph Carson, who responded in the usual way: by cracking down on vice. A new slot machine ordinance and a couple of high-profile arrests in 1933 and 1934 put a lot of pressure on Enloe's operation. During his 1934 trial, he declared himself a pauper, having put all of his assets in his wife's name. By 1937, Enloe's wife was divorcing him, taking all of his assets with her, and Enloe was drinking heavily. Elkins, sensing Enloe's weakness, went after his slot machine operation. Armed with a pistol, shotgun and a lead-weighted glove, Elkins and his accomplices began raiding businesses that used Enloe's slot machines, intimidating the customers and stealing the machines.

Huerth describes a dramatic confrontation between Elkins and Enloe in which Elkins informed the older man that he was taking over his business. He might already have had control at that point because, in November 1937, Elkins's Washington County warehouse was raided, and police found between two hundred and three hundred slot machines. Although the machines themselves weren't illegal at that point, the police seized them as stolen property. The raid was prompted by a robbery at a Hillsboro tavern. When sheriff's deputies arrived, Elkins and his accomplice, Herbert West, fired at them. Both men were arrested and charged with armed robbery. A rent receipt in Elkins's pocket led the sheriff to the stash of stolen slot machines. Elkins and West were acquitted of the robbery charges. There is no record of what happened to the slot machines, but after the incident, Elkins was the new "slot machine king," and Enloe was on the downward slide that ended in his death in 1945.

Rumors said that Elkins had connections to the Los Angeles crime syndicate through mobster Mickey Cohen, an associate of Benjamin "Bugsy" Siegel. Elkins usually didn't bother denying the charges; he just gave his usual chilly smile. He clearly had some kind of connections, though, because criminal charges never stuck to him. He was arrested twice in 1938 on narcotics charges, once in Seattle and once in Portland on a warrant out of San Francisco. The Seattle case went nowhere, but in the fall of 1938, he was extradited to San Francisco to face federal charges of moving a large shipment of heroin and morphine from San Francisco to Portland. Conviction on the federal charges drew a fifteen-month sentence, but Elkins spent only about a year in Leavenworth Prison before returning to Portland in 1940. According to Huerth, Elkins already had strong influence with the city in 1937. By 1940, he had strengthened those ties by paying tribute to Al Winter, who had strong ties to city councilman Earl Riley and by recruiting a young police detective with promising prospects: Jim Purcell.

4

BUSINESS AS USUAL

The real prostitutes…in Portland are the prostitutes in office.
—*Governor Oswald West*

Portland's city government had been run for the benefit of the powerful and influential for more than eighty years when Joseph Carson was elected mayor in 1932. The outgoing mayor, George Baker, had been in office since 1917, serving four terms and becoming Portland's longest-serving mayor. Baker, a former actor and theater manager, was a popular and affable man who joined every imaginable organization from the Elks to the Ku Klux Klan and was known as the "kissin' mayor" for his enthusiastic greeting of female visitors. On one memorable occasion when Queen Marie of Romania visited Portland, Baker patted her on the ass. Baker, who had grown up in poverty, identified with "the man in the street" and used his image to great advantage. As a downtown theater manager, though, his sympathies were with the business class, who dominated the Arlington Club and the city government. Baker believed in government by and for a network of "good-old-boys" who socialized together and did business together seamlessly. Baker's cronies, known as the "city hall crowd," had exclusive, no-bid contracts for city insurance, construction and other services. One member of the city hall crowd was J.J. Parker, a former poolhall operator who was well on his way to owning all of the first-run movie theaters in town. Alcohol was illegal in Portland during all four of Baker's mayoral administrations, but Baker and the "city hall crowd" had no trouble getting a drink. The evidence room at

Mayor George Baker, the kissin' mayor, was Portland's longest-serving mayor, filling four terms from 1917 until 1933. His handsome, paternalistic image was perfect for booming economic times, but by 1932, his popularity was fading. Photographer unknown. *Courtesy of the Portland City Archive 2012-30.*

the Central Precinct, where alcohol seized from bootleggers was stored, was their private liquor cabinet.

The police bureau became quite efficient at enforcing the Prohibition laws for any entrepreneurs who tried to compete with the "approved" bootleggers. It enforced them so well that the price of booze in Portland was the highest on the West Coast. Bobby Evans rose to the top of the heap of bootleggers in Portland. From the Shamrock Athletic Club, Evans's combination gym and cigar store on Southwest Second Avenue, he collected protection money from bootleggers and criminals who moonlighted as bootleggers, such as "Shy Frank" Kodat, who ran a burglary/armed robbery ring from his speakeasy on Southeast Water Street; Tom Johnson, who had inherited Yam Wallace's network of railroad porter/smugglers and sold his bonded whiskey at the Golden West Hotel and other places; and the DePinto brothers—Nick, Mike and Ray—who ran several joints downtown but who were mostly interested in pimping and strong-arm work.

There was always room for imaginative entrepreneurs, such as the woman who ran the Morrison Hotel (the one downtown, not on the east side). The run-down hotel rented rooms by the hour or by the night. Each room had a bottle of booze in one of the dresser drawers, and you could always arrange for company if you wanted. When the place was raided in 1925 (somebody must have missed a payment), the police found a lot of men who said they were there to "meet a friend." The police could be very helpful in getting a prospective businessperson set up. Virginia Washburne, who went undercover in Portland to investigate Prohibition enforcement for the Anti-Saloon League, claimed that a cop in St. Johns showed her where she could bring liquor in by boat and offered to help her find a place to rent so she could sell her product. Similarly, Bobby Evans effectively helped many would-be bootleggers get started. He liked to attend "smokers" with the mayor and was popular among the city hall crowd because of his earlier career as a boxer. According to Floyd Marsh, the city payoff from liquor alone ran to $100,000 a month.

Baker's alliance with organized criminals was nothing new in Portland. In the 1890s, Joseph Simon, boss of the Republican political machine, allied with Larry Sullivan, the sailors' boardinghouse operator who ran the North End, and Frank Woon, who controlled vice in Chinatown with his army of "highbinders." In return for protection from police interference in their operations, Sullivan and Woon provided votes, both legal and illegal. Even Bobby Evans had a predecessor in Jonathan Bourne, the flamboyant man-about-town who worked to ensure the connection between the government and the underworld in the 1890s and 1900s. George Baker, a man conservative to the core, refined the relationship by organizing for highest efficiency. Baker's efficient system worked well as long as there was plenty of money. His handsome, paternalistic image was perfect for the economic boom Portland experienced during the Great War and the first part of the 1920s. By the end of the '20s, and Baker's last term as mayor, things had changed, and the "kissin' mayor" was not as popular as he had been.

The Public Market Scandal of 1932 was the final straw. Plans for the huge concrete building that was to go up between Front Street and the river, where Tom McCall Waterfront Park is today, had been in process for nearly five years. Originally conceived as a way to get the congested and messy Yamhill Public Market off the streets, the location was chosen because the property was owned by Julius Meier, who would soon be governor, and the William Ladd Estate controlled by Frederick Strong, one of the city hall crowd. Failing banks and falling property values held the project up for years, but in 1932, the city finally agreed to purchase the land so it could move forward. Baker and the city council agreed to pay $480,000 for the property, even though its assessed value was only $280,000. Outraged at the overpayment, Portland voters became even angrier when rumors circulated that the mayor and several council members had accepted bribes in order to approve the deal. The Recall Election of 1932 was meant to be a clean sweep, but thanks to a timely burglary pulled off by Bobby Evans's organization, Councilman Earl Riley and District Attorney Lotus Langley were spared. Councilman John Mann was recalled by more than two-thirds of the vote. Approximately 47 percent of the voters wanted to recall Baker, and he knew his days were numbered.

The recall election occurred in April 1932. In November, the city would elect a mayor and two city council members. Mayor Baker read the handwriting on the wall and declined to run for reelection to a fifth term. The voters were in a foul mood, and no members of the city government were willing to face them as a candidate for mayor. The year 1932 was the worst one of the Great Depression, and between the recall election and the general election, Portlanders witnessed the debacle of the Bonus Expeditionary Army (BEA), which began organizing in the squatter Hoovervilles of East Portland. What began as a local protest movement by Great War veterans soon turned into a national movement. Homeless veterans from all over the country gathered in Washington, D.C., to demand bonus money that they had been promised by the United States Congress. For many of the participants of the Bonus March, the pittance that had been promised them was the only hope they had for supporting their families. In July, President Herbert Hoover ordered the army, under the command of Colonel Douglas McArthur, to clear the protestors out of their encampment at Anacostia Flats. Two of the protestors were killed in the confrontation, and Hoover's hope of reelection died with them. Franklin

The Seawall Public Market was a popular idea that became the center of a scandal over graft and corruption that nearly brought down Mayor Baker's administration. City councilman Earl Riley, implicated in the scandal, survived to become mayor in 1941. Photograph by Arthur Rothstein. *Courtesy of the Library of Congress.*

Delano Roosevelt, with his promise of averting revolution by instituting radical change, was poised to take over.

No members of the city government were willing to run for mayor, but nearly everyone else was. There were more than fifteen candidates for mayor in the November election, the most in any Portland city election until 2000, ranging from the conservative state senator William Woodward to the Communist party organizer Dirk DeJonge. Anna Schrader, former private detective, professional swimmer and the focus of a scandal involving graft and illicit sexual relationships in the police bureau, carried on a brief campaign for mayor. She had been active in efforts to expose graft in the police bureau and in city government recall elections in 1930 and 1932, but her name was not included on the official ballot for mayor. Since 1913, the city offices had been "non-partisan," but party affiliation was usually well known. The candidates in 1932 filled the spectrum of the Republican Party, from the liberal, "wet" candidate L.B. Sandblast; through the chamber of commerce's candidate, Frank Shull; to the right-wing candidate Robert Duncan. Only two candidates represented the Democratic Party on the ballot: Elton Watkins, former United States representative and unsuccessful candidate for the Senate in 1930, and Joseph Carson, an ambitious attorney from Hood River who had run three unsuccessful races for the state legislature.

Carson, a conservative pro-business Democrat, was known for his emotional rhetorical style and for his frequent emphasis on "Americanism." His speeches were rousing in a style that has gone out of fashion since the 1930s. In one memorable speech during the Waterfront Strike of 1934, Carson waved the bloodstained shirt of J.E. Bateson, a strikebreaker accidently killed in a confrontation between special police officers and striking picketers. The emotional appeal lost Carson the respect of many working-class Portlanders and won him the derogatory nickname "Bloody Shirt" Carson. He appeared on stage with Franklin Roosevelt when FDR made a campaign stop in Portland, associating himself with the popular presidential candidate. Roosevelt's coattails might have been partly responsible for Carson's victory in the election, but Carson was no New Deal Democrat. With no experience in government or administration, Carson was not prepared for the daunting job that faced the mayor of a city with more than 100,000 people who were out of work and dependant on relief programs. Despite a well-publicized "learning vacation" in Hawaii before taking office in January 1933, Carson governed the city in an emotional style that constantly reacted to events and tried to deal with situations when they became emergencies. He did a good enough job to get reelected in 1936, and the verdict of historians such as E. Kimbark MacColl and Jewel Lansing is that he did his best in a bad situation.

There was more than one recall petition circulated against Carson during his two terms in office, but they usually revolved around his inept performance or his blatantly political use of power rather than charges of corruption. Carson had a cozy relationship with the business community, especially the chamber of commerce, and "sweetheart deals" involving insurance purchases and construction and service contracts continued in the manner that had always prevailed. Carson didn't have overt relationships

The Portland Police Bureau Vice Squad was tasked with enforcing laws against drinking, gambling and prostitution. In reality, they worked as enforcers for the "approved" vice operations, enforcing the laws against competitors. Photographer unknown. *Courtesy of the Portland Police Historical Society*.

with gangsters, as his predecessor George Baker and his successor Earl Riley did, but the payoff continued. It was not unusual for people in the top jobs to be left "out of the loop" where payoffs were concerned. For example, police chief Leon Jenkins might not have participated in the payoff from Prohibition gangsters as he claimed, although Anna Schrader disputed the claim, but his underlings in the police department participated fully, hiding the truth from the selectively blind chief. That might have been the case with Mayor Carson as well. Either way, with the power vacuum in Portland's underworld that existed after 1932, the payoff was bound to be less formal and systematic.

Although alcohol was legal after Carson's first year in office, Oregon's restrictive liquor laws left lots of opportunities for bootleggers. For example, it was illegal to sell liquor by the drink. People going out for an evening of nightclubbing would have to purchase a bottle at the state-owned Green Front stores and then pay the bartender to serve it to them through the evening. The Green Front stores closed early, so anyone who wanted to drink late was a potential customer for bootleggers. Most of the city's taxi drivers could help their thirsty customers find a bottle after hours, though. Many of them, like Jack Minsky, were involved in prostitution operations as well, so they served as all-around vice caterers. Tom Johnson kept his well-organized railroad operation going, supplying after-hours clubs with untaxed, high-quality whiskey from Canada. He wasn't the only one. The "speakeasy culture" of Prohibition was transforming into the "nightclub culture" that would not really take off until the Depression ended.

The police bureau's vice squad, commanded by Captain John Keegan, was tasked with enforcing the city's laws concerning alcohol, prostitution and gambling. Keegan used the Vice Squad to eliminate competition for "unauthorized" vice operators. "Authorized" vice operators paid for protection and were left in peace. Marie L. John, a Chinatown shop owner, claimed that she had paid Detective Horace Harms of the Vice Squad $300 a week for protection of her slot machine and lottery side business. Harms denied the charges but then was quietly removed from the police bureau. Burton Lawson, Carson's Great War commander, took over as police chief

Mayors Joseph Carson (center) and Earl Riley (to Carson's left) ran Portland in the manner of Mayor George Baker, collecting payoffs from vice operators and rewarding their supporters with valuable city contracts. Photographer unknown. *Courtesy of the Portland City Archive A2011-004.22.*

when Carson took office. He seemed to be sincere in his desire to clean up the bureau, but he often complained that the cop on the beat could find gambling games but the chief could not. Accusations of graft against the chief arose during the waterfront strike, but it was his handling of the trigger-happy special police and his confrontational style that forced him to resign shortly after. His successor, Harry Niles, was a longtime policeman who was nearing seventy. Excellent at public relations, Niles improved the image of the police bureau but had little energy or patience for trying to stop graft.

Carson continued his emotional harangues on Americanism and rousing attacks on Communism and Socialism during his two terms as mayor. He participated fully in Governor Martin's Red Scare and used the police bureau's Red Squad, also commanded by Captain Keegan, to attack his political opponents. Carson developed a clandestine relationship with the Teamsters' Union, infiltrated by Red Squad provocateurs who were interested in earning money from criminal enterprises as much as fighting Communism. The Red Squad also urged and used violent tactics during the Waterfront Strike, the Beer Wars and the Goon War to degrade the image of unions and to sow dissension among them. Unions, such as the Teamsters' and the Sailors' Union of the Pacific, attacked radical members, forcing them out of the unions. Carson's emotional, reactive rhetorical style and condoning—and even advocating—violence directly influenced the level of political and labor violence in Portland during the 1930s.

It must have been a relief when longtime city councilman R. Earl Riley was elected mayor in 1940. Riley, a protégée of George Baker and the first Portland native to be elected mayor, took office as the economy began to improve and Portland became an important center of shipbuilding again. Riley, while just as anti-Communist and pro-American as Mayor Carson, was a much cooler politician. In place of Carson's emotional rhetorical style, Riley was a boring speaker. His terms as mayor were a return to the "good old boy" style of government that had been highly popular in the days of Mayor Baker. Riley was directly involved with the payoff, personally handling about $60,000 a month, which he kept locked in a secret vault he had installed in his city hall office. Historian E. Kimbark MacColl was shown the vault and told about the payoff by Riley's successor, Dorothy McCullough Lee. Riley was able to systematize the payoff through his childhood friend Al Winter, who by 1940 dominated the vice industry from his extremely popular Pago Pago Room nightclub. On December 7, 1941, less than a year into Riley's first term as mayor, opportunities to organize and systematize graft and vice increased greatly with wartime conditions.

5
THE GOOD WAR AT HOME

Vice is a condition that exists in every large city. We have good people and we have
bad people, and sometimes I wonder if the sinners are not in the majority…Law
enforcement cannot rise above decided public demand and public cooperation.
—*Judge Walter L. Tooze*

World War II had a profound effect on Portland. The city saw some of
its most important changes as it became one of the major shipbuilding
centers in the United States. Housing shortages, rising wages and prices and
social tensions dominated the period from 1939 to 1945, but national unity
on the war, especially after the bombing of Pearl Harbor, forced social issues
onto the back burner. Those long-delayed confrontations would take on new
importance after the war, but for about six years, they just simmered. New
opportunities abounded. For workers, higher wages, more job choices and
greater protection for unions improved their lives. Most unions signed "no
strike pledges" for the duration of the war, so an uneasy peace dominated
labor. Racial and gender discrimination in the workplace, and even within
the unions, would continue to be a problem, but those issues would take a
back seat to the effort to win the war as well. At the same time, social problems
and racial divides in neighborhoods and communities were intensified by the
shortage of housing in the city and the low quality of the housing that was
hastily built to meet wartime needs. Wartime rationing of alcohol, gasoline,
meat and other necessities increased opportunities for organized crime. The
perceived need for added security on the waterfront and in the shipyards
gave criminals the chance to build legitimacy and strengthen their ties to

Acute housing shortages in 1941 prompted Henry Kaiser to develop and build Vanport, the country's largest public housing development and Oregon's second-largest city. Photographer unknown. *Courtesy of the Portland City Archive A201-025.626.*

local and national government. The round-the-clock shifts at the shipyards turned Portland into a twenty-four-hour town. Restaurants, nightclubs and movie theaters began to operate at all hours.

The changes began before the United States entered the war. By the time Pearl Harbor was bombed in December 1941, the Kaiser Shipyards in Vancouver, Swan Island and St. Johns were already in operation, pumping out "liberty ships" at record-breaking rates. Henry Kaiser and his son Edgar had already broken ground on Vanport, just outside the city limits. Portland, which had been resisting public housing for more than a decade, would soon find itself next to the largest public housing project in the nation. Within two years, there would be major public housing developments inside the city as well, at Guild's Lake and Columbia Villa. The boom in public housing came in response to the explosive growth of Portland's population. The Hoovervilles at the east end of the Ross Island Bridge and in Sullivan's Gulch overflowed. New shantytowns grew along Interstate and Union Avenues as the city absorbed more than 100,000 new residents; this was a population increase in excess of 30 percent.

Portland, known as the most racist city in the West, would see its racial makeup changed forever as twenty thousand new African American residents settled in its segregated neighborhoods. Portland's small, active black community, which numbered about two thousand in 1940, was overwhelmed by the newcomers. Many black Portlanders had learned that "keeping their place" could lead to financial opportunity and stability and hadn't yet begun to act on the realization that their new numbers could help them improve that "place." Unofficial policies of segregated housing confined the new African American residents to the area along North Williams Avenue and to specific neighborhoods in Vanport and the other public housing developments. Tom Johnson, the African American bootlegger, became the city's first black real estate agent and the only one who would sell or rent to blacks. Johnson's Keystone Investments office was next door to his Keystone Club; entertainment and vice went hand in hand in his business plan. By the end of the war, Williams Avenue, lined with nightclubs, was known as Black Broadway. Portland was a major venue for jazz musicians, earning the city a new nickname: Jumptown.

Amidst the city's wartime growth, the Portland Police Bureau was a demoralized force. What had been decent pay at the beginning of the Depression had been frozen for a decade, and the only hope for a living wage came from payoffs and graft. Retirement held out no hope with the pathetic benefit of thirty dollars per month, so aging officers clung desperately to their jobs. Police chief Harry Niles was over seventy years old himself and had little interest in improving the force or its performance. Under Chief Leon Jenkins and his successor, Niles, the police bureau had been very progressive in its use of technology but remained reactionary in its personnel and labor policies.

Chief Jenkins had set up one of the first fingerprint and forensic evidence departments in the country, as well as introducing both motorcycle and automobile patrols. Chief Niles introduced education requirements for patrol officers, the first use of radio communications in an American police force and airplane patrols. Harry Niles's genius, though, was in public relations. His tireless efforts in that field, including weekly broadcasts over KGW radio, had improved the police bureau's image considerably. Reality, however, lagged far behind the image. Low pay; the old idea of "pay for service," which had been a part of Portland policing since the 1850s; and peer pressure made graft a persistent problem, especially on Captain Keegan's

Frank Springer joined the Portland Police Bureau in 1938. He was one of the founding members of the first chartered police union in the country and worked tirelessly to reform the police bureau and its image during a thirty-five-year career. Photographer unknown. *Courtesy of the Portland Police Historical Society.*

Vice Squad. Drinking on the job was accepted, even expected, for members of the Vice Squad, and suicide was a serious problem. Nearly every member of the police bureau knew at least one officer who had killed himself, often after a stint on the Vice Squad. Many officers joined the bureau for idealistic reasons that could not survive the daily reality of corruption, use of the police for political ends, long hours and low pay.

The most spectacular police suicide of the period occurred on May 9, 1941, in the Eastside Precinct headquarters in the old Water Bureau building on Southeast Seventh Avenue and Alder Street. Officer Arthur Chase was a veteran of more than twenty years in the police bureau at the time, but his career had passed him by. With no hope of advancement, Chase was still a beat cop when he was one of rookie Frank Springer's trainers. According to Springer, Chase was a good trainer, but he was seized by severe depression and bitter resentment for his supervisor, Lieutenant Phillip Johnson of the night relief. Johnson and Chase had been partners back in the 1920s when Johnson began an affair with Chase's wife. Chase's wife fell in love with Johnson and divorced her husband. Johnson, who was looking for a lover not a wife, promptly dumped her. Chase, hurt by the divorce, still loved his ex-wife and couldn't forgive Johnson for insulting her. Somehow, the two ex-partners were assigned to the same shift, with Johnson in command. Springer says that things were tense at the precinct house, as neither man would speak to the other. One night, Chase arrived late for roll call, and Johnson suspended him. A suspension required a hearing, and Chase's was set for May 9. Chase arrived at the precinct house about 3:00 a.m. armed with two pistols. He opened fire as soon as he saw Johnson and chased him into a back office, where he killed his ex-partner. Chase then jumped in his car and drove to his childhood home on the Clackamas River, where he shot himself.

By the summer of 1941, about one-third of the police bureau was over age or in poor physical condition. Unable to survive on the meager pension available, most officers stayed on the job long after they were capable of doing it. Mayor Riley and Chief Niles came up with an innovative plan to relieve the problem—Portland officers would be ranked by physical fitness. The one hundred officers ranked the lowest would be assigned to walking beats in Portland parks and transferred to the parks department at the reduced salary of $100 per month. The reduction in manpower would be covered by making the rest of the officers work twelve-hour shifts. What was seen as a form of pension by the city was viewed as a severe punishment by rank and file officers. The final straw came on December 8, 1941, the day after the bombing of Pearl Harbor, when Mayor Riley announced that "days off" would be suspended in the police bureau for the duration of the war. Military enlistments soon reduced the bureau's manpower further, and many of the "Park Patrol" returned to duty with a new bitterness against their employer.

During the Park Patrol controversy, Officer John D. Hayes approached friends at the Labor Temple about the need for a "policemen's union." The idea of organizing police was very controversial, as many labor activists felt that the police, whom they often saw as natural enemies, couldn't legally join unions. After the suspension of "days off," the Central Labor Council voted to assign two organizers, S.P. Stevens and Fred Gleichman, to the task. An underground "authorization card" campaign began before the end of the year. On April 14, 1942, an open organizational meeting held at Norse Hall on the east side drew Frank Springer and 209 other officers, more than 60 percent of the force. In May, the American Federation of State, County and Municipal Employees (AFSCME) chartered the Portland Police Association (PPA) Local 456 as the first chartered "police union" in the country.

Labor unions had come a long way since the bloody days of 1934. The violence of the 1930s subsided into the uneasy peace of the fight against fascism. United States propaganda played up the contrast between the free labor of America and the slave labor of the Nazi and Japanese empires. Labor unions, enjoying an unprecedented legitimacy and legal status, participated fully. One of the oldest of the craft unions was the Sailors' Union of the Pacific (SUP), founded in San Francisco in 1885. The SUP was not only one of the oldest unions on the West Coast, but it was also

The heroic story of the Merchant Marine agency during World War II has not been thoroughly told. Suffering a higher casualty rate than any other service except the Marine Corps, Merchant Marines were considered civilians and received limited GI Bill benefits. Artist: Glenn Stuart Pearce. *Courtesy of the Library of Congress.*

considered one of the most radical and toughest unions in the country. Affiliated with the International Seamen's Union (ISU) of the AF of L, the West Coast sailors firmly maintained their independence and fought for the rights of their members, who were some of the most oppressed workers in the United States at the time. From the 1860s well into the 1920s, sailors were excluded from Constitutional rights and subjected to a legal system of debt slavery that was overseen by a class of criminals known as Crimps. Onboard ships, the captains had immense power to punish sailors for infractions that sometimes included execution. The SUP had to be tough in order to survive. It was not unusual for its organizing methods to become violent. In 1893, a bombing in San Francisco was blamed on the SUP. In a gruesome case from Aberdeen, Washington, in 1910 the *Oregonian* speculated that there could be as many as thirty-three bodies in the cold waters of Gray's Harbor and the Chehalis River, put there by SUP business agent William Gohl and other members of the union. In a bloody battle with Communists among their membership and the East Coast–based ISU, the SUP was expelled from the AF of L in 1936.

Violent it might have been, but unlike some unions, racism was not a failing of the SUP. In 1942, when West Coast Japanese residents were rounded up in compliance with the president's internment order, the SUP complained that "35–40 ethnic-Japanese members" had been interned in the stables at the Santa Anita Racetrack although they had proved their loyalty as union members. After a fight, the government finally gave in, releasing the Japanese American sailors for work in the Atlantic Merchant Marine. The heroic story of the Merchant Marine in World War II has not been told enough. Suffering a casualty rate higher than any United States service during the war except the Marine Corps, merchant sailors—many of them members of the SUP—never received full veteran benefits because they held "union jobs." United States Navy sailors who survived sinking vessels were paid for every day they served in uniform. Survivors of merchant vessels lost their contracts, and their pay, when the ships sunk. And sink they did—that's why the Portland shipyards had to pump out new ships so fast.

Sinking was just one of the dangers that merchant sailors faced. Sailors of the liberty ship *Jean Nicolet*, in 1944, faced summary execution or attempted escape through shark-infested waters after being sunk and captured by a Japanese submarine. Twenty-three made it out alive from a crew of one hundred who survived the sinking. In 1942, the *Stephen Hopkins*, under the command of Captain Paul Buck, with August "Sails" Reese, a veteran Cape Horn sailor and Portland SUP member aboard, faced down the notorious German *Raider J*. The fast, heavily armed German raider *Tannenfells* had been on a months-long voyage that had already claimed twenty-six liberty ships. In October 1942, it rendezvoused with the lightly armed freighter *Steirs* in

Liberty ships provided supplies for troops all over the world during the war and were a prime target for German and Japanese raiders. The urgent need for these ships kept Portland's three shipyards humming twenty-four hours a day. Photograph by Carol Highsmith. *Courtesy of the Library of Congress.*

the south Atlantic to transfer prisoners. The *Stephen Hopkins*, four days out of Cape Town and "sailing light"—without cargo—for Brazil stumbled on the two ships. Captain Buck, who would soon have a liberty ship named after him, had vowed that if he encountered a German raider, he would fight. Armed with a few machine guns and an obsolete four-inch gun, the merchant sailors and a small United States Naval Reserve guard fought the two German ships to a standstill in a bloody battle. The *Steirs* and the *Stephen Hopkins* sank. The *Tannenfels* was badly damaged and had to limp home, ending its raiding career. Out of the hundred-man crew of the *Stephen Hopkins*, fifteen made it to Brazil after a week at sea in a single lifeboat, partly due to the old-time sailing experience of Sails Reese. On the "Murmansk Run," delivering supplies to our Soviet allies, merchant sailors identified as "Trotskeyites" by the GPU secret police sometimes disappeared into Stalin's gulag system.

Along with the dangers facing sailors, racism was a persistent issue in many of the maritime unions. Both the AF of L and the CIO banned discrimination "on the basis of race, creed or color" in their affiliated unions, but the practices of the local unions were not monitored and varied widely. A 1945 survey of fourteen Portland local unions found that eight admitted African Americans as full members. The other six excluded blacks, but two of them, including the Boilermakers and Shipbuilders Union, had "auxiliary locals" that allowed African American members without giving them full rights. Of the eight unions that admitted blacks, most had miniscule black memberships, blaming the lack of African Americans on a lack of skills or on hostility from white workers and employers. Building Workers Union (BWU) Local 296, which organized janitors, porters and handymen, had more than 2,000 black members, out of a total membership of 5,500, and claimed "that there are no interracial problems in the union and…some of the best workers are Negroes." Other unions, like the Electrical Workers' Union and the Carpenters' Union, admitted black members but noted that employers often wouldn't keep them on the job and sometimes white union members refused to work with them. The Laundry Workers' Union and the International Longshore and Warehouse Union experienced "wildcat strikes" or work stoppages by white members when they attempted to put African American members to work.

Nationally, A. Philip Randolph, Bayard Rustin and other civil rights leaders were determined not to make the mistake of World War I, letting civil rights wait until the war was over. Instead, they waged a "Double V" (victory) campaign under the slogan: "Defeat Hitler, Mussolini and Hirohito by Abolishing Jim Crow." A threatened "Negro march" on Washington prompted President Roosevelt to issue Executive Order 8802 in 1941, banning racial discrimination in defense industries and government jobs and setting up the Fair Employment Practices Commission (FEPC). The fact that Roosevelt also issued Executive Order 9346 in 1943, saying pretty much the same thing, shows how difficult the fight for civil rights was during the war. In Portland, noted as the only city on the West Coast with "White Trade Only" signs in restaurant windows, discrimination was a reality that white citizens tended to deny. The official position of the Housing Authority of Portland (HAP) was: "We don't discriminate, but we do segregate." Rising numbers and increased competition for work as the wartime boom wound down, combined with routine police violence against African Americans, led black Portlanders to new political organizing efforts. In response to the police shooting of Ervin Jones in his Guild's Lake home in 1945, Dr. DeNorval Unthank and other prominent African American citizens founded a Portland chapter of the Urban League, bringing organizer Bill Berry from Chicago to run the group. While Berry and his staff did pioneer work in integrating employment opportunities, he reflected the Portland attitude when outlining his goal to help "decent, hard-working and self-respecting colored people." Portlanders, both black and white, could agree on one thing: they wanted the newcomers to go home. Most of them weren't going anywhere, though.

Jim Elkins was one new Portlander who was here to stay. Elkins returned to Portland in late 1940, after his federal incarceration, and went back to work. He founded the Service Machine Company as a front for his vending machine and slot machine operation and quickly dominated the heroin trade, bootleg liquor and burglary. Coincidentally, "Shy Frank" Kodat, who had dominated burglary in the northwest for nearly twenty years, went to prison for the last time in 1940. That was a fate that befell many of Elkins's enemies as he cooperated with state and local authorities in order to eliminate his rivals. Wartime security fears gave Elkins new opportunities as he cooperated with the United States Coast Guard and Naval Intelligence to provide "protection" for shipping and shipbuilding facilities. Wartime rationing provided even more opportunities. Liquor was rationed to one bottle per month, and "by the drink" sale had remained illegal when Prohibition ended. Tight gas rationing opened even more bootlegging opportunities. A gas station at Southeast Tenth Avenue and Powell Boulevard was reported to be receiving after-dark deliveries of bootleg gasoline from Canada. The men's room at Al Winter's Pago Pago Club was a good place to buy black market "gas stamps" at the unheard of price of one dollar per gallon.

Jim Elkins was involved in all of it. When his Service Machine Company office on Southwest Second Avenue was raided in 1944, Oregon Liquor Control Commission (OLCC) agents found thirty-five gallons of illegal booze, plus gallons of gasoline and black market tires and inner tubes hidden under a woodpile. The OLCC was the one agency that was willing to go after Elkins at the time because he was a major participant in the "payoff" of city, county and state officials. Even the federal Office of Price Administration (OPA), tasked with enforcing rationing and wage and price legislation, left Elkins alone, possibly because of his cooperation with the coast guard and navy. Elkins always claimed that he was not involved in prostitution, but it was his brother Fred's specialty, and "Big Jim" collected protection from, and employed, brothel owners. Prostitution was a booming business. In 1939, the city made brothels along Northwest Third Avenue remove their prominent neon signs, and in 1942, the air force closed sixty-two brothels in Portland when the Portland Training Airbase opened and three thousand recruits poured into the area. Venereal disease rates soared as enterprising young women created a home-based industry, and undercover brothels opened in neighborhoods all over Portland and Vanport.

Armed robbery was another booming industry. Many jobs were pulled by amateurs, a lot of them AWOL soldiers, sailors or airmen. Those jobs often ended with murder victims, such as Walter Poole. He was shot to death on Christmas Eve 1945; robbed of his car, some cash and a ring; and left in front of a partially dismantled apartment building in Vanport. Wardell Henderson, a black AWOL soldier, was convicted and executed for his murder. There were at least two gangs of organized robbers working in Portland during the war. One was Jim Elkins's gang, which chose vice operators and other criminals for its victims. Roy Moore's gang, on the other hand, concentrated on payroll robberies, usually with big payoffs. It isn't clear who was behind the Joe Mezzina job. Moore's gang took the heat, but Mezzina was an Elkins-style target.

Joe Mezzina, an Italian immigrant, came to Portland in the early 1920s. Not much is known about his background, but it was a time when the New Orleans mob was colonizing West Coast cities, setting up syndicates in Los Angeles, San Francisco, San Jose and Seattle. It is not clear whether Mezzina was connected to any organization, but his business was restaurants and his specialties were bootlegging, gambling and pornography. Mezzina survived a long series of arrests before establishing himself as one of the "colorful" downtown restaurateurs. Mezzina put up a macho front and usually carried a handgun, which he was not afraid to use. He used it on December 3, 1944, when two ex-convicts tried to rob him on his way home from work. Carrying $840 in cash and "hundreds of dollars" in checks, Mezzina was accosted at the front door of his eastside apartment house. Instead of money, he gave the robbers lead. W.E. Bennett, a local strong-arm man, was killed. George "Killer" Frederick wounded Mezzina before being badly wounded himself.

The main connection to Moore's gang was Oscar Thomas, a safecracker who loaned his car to the robbers. Roy Moore had been the "king of the northwest bootleggers" when he was sent to federal prison in 1929, but he had been an armed robber from the start. He and his partner, Bert Orcutt, robbed the Sells-Floto Circus in Vancouver, Washington, in 1921. Two years at McNeil Island Penitentiary for bootlegging and the end of Prohibition sent Moore back to his roots. Returning to Portland in 1932, Moore financed his gambling addiction with his armed robbery ring. In December 1945, Moore and his gang pulled off a triple robbery in Brownsville, Oregon, robbing the town hardware store, pharmacy and grocery store all on the same day. Escaping with $20,000 in war bonds and more than $8,000 in cash, the robbers had a falling out by the time they reached Portland. Ernest Bowman, a drifter from Kelso, Washington, was killed. Moore had to take it on the lam and would return to Oregon in 1952 to be sentenced to life in prison as a "habitual criminal." By then, Joe Mezzina was long dead.

The restaurateur was gunned down in his place, Joe's Lunch on Southwest Third Avenue, on November 10, 1945. He insisted on prosecuting George Frederick for attempted murder in the 1944 attack and was scheduled to testify at his trial on November 12. Shortly after midnight on the tenth, Joe Mezzina was closing up his combination cardroom/tavern when a young gunman accosted him. Mezzina winked at barmaid Arletta Pitner before pulling his pistol and being shot between the eyes. Other witnesses watched the killer flee down Southwest Third Avenue and through the Plaza Blocks. Within minutes of the killing, police arrested Alfred Reed (also known as Joe Walker), who had been Frederick's cellmate at the Washington State Penitentiary in Walla Walla. Reed was an enforcer for Moore's gang, and no charges were brought against him. In December, police in Spokane arrested Harold Wayne Hollister (also known as Bert Crenshaw) for a tavern robbery. Hollister, a paratrooper in Africa and Italy, had been discharged at Fort Lewis in October 1945. In an eerie parallel of the death penalty case of Wardell Henderson, circumstantial evidence tied the troubled veteran to the crime, and soon he confessed to the killing. Like Henderson, he repudiated his confession and then pleaded insanity, but Hollister, who was white, was sentenced to life in prison instead of execution.

Along with criminal activity in general came a dramatic rise in juvenile delinquency. One explanation was the increasing number of women entering the workforce, leaving adolescents on their own. It was not just the children of working-class and poor people who were tempted to juvenile delinquency, though. John J. Parker III was the son of J.J. Parker, the theater magnate who, at one time, had owned all of the first-run movie houses in town. By 1941, he still owned some of the biggest and best theaters, including the Broadway, the Music Box, the Mayfair and the United Artists. In August 1941, J.J. Parker died of a heart attack while on vacation in Seaside. His son was sixteen. Two months later, Orson Welles's masterpiece film *Citizen Kane* opened at J.J. Parker's Broadway Theater. The impressionable teenager, already a movie fan, was greatly influenced by the film. He started planning his own films and finally, in 1947, persuaded his mother, Hazel Parker, "the First Lady of Portland Theater," to open the Guild Theater on Southwest Park Avenue as a venue for foreign and art films. By that time, John J. Parker III was already running with a bad crowd, spending time in the dives along Burnside Street

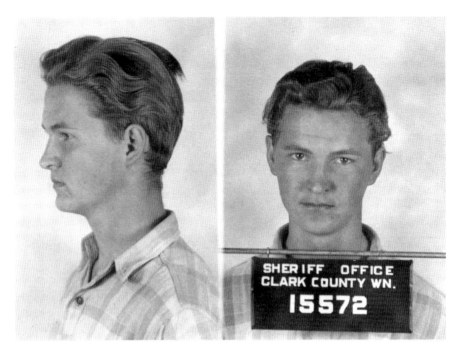

Utah Wilson came from a family affected by incest. His father went to jail for that crime when Utah was two. Utah was arrested for his first burglary when he was eight. By then, three of his brothers had gone to prison for rape. Photographer unknown. *Courtesy of the Walter Graven Estate.*

and experimenting with drugs. At least one young woman claimed that he got her hooked on Benzedrine and pressured her into prostitution.

Poor kids were tempted into juvenile delinquency as well. Large families from the rural Midwest, who came to Portland escaping the Dust Bowl conditions that destroyed their homes, provided plenty of poor kids. Most of them found work in the shipyards or lumber mills, but some of them were not interested in working for a living. Mose Wilson brought his family from Kansas in the late 1920s and settled in a rural area near Camas, Washington. In 1933, Wilson was convicted of incest with his thirteen-year-old daughter and went to the Washington State Penitentiary, leaving his wife alone to raise eight children. In dire poverty, and with little adult supervision, the Wilson kids ran wild. Grant Wilson, one of two Wilsons without a criminal record, remembered a Christmas when he was little when his older brothers piled presents under the family tree. Grant knew that they had stolen the presents, but he was glad to have the holiday. Lester, the only other Wilson boy with no criminal record, served in the United States Army and died during the invasion of Sicily in 1943. By then, most of his brothers were in jail.

The eldest Wilson brother, Rassi, took a job at the Kaiser shipyard in Vancouver, but he was directing his younger brothers in a series of burglaries and armed robberies that terrorized tavern, grocery store and service station owners all over Portland and southwest Washington. Utah, the youngest Wilson brother, was arrested for his first burglary when he was eight years old and spent some time in the Washington State Reform School at Chehalis before he escaped. The other two brothers, Glenn and Turman, joined their elder brother in a series of rapes in 1942. The three brothers were arrested after the abduction and rape of two high school girls in St. Johns and a shootout with Portland police officers. Rassi was sentenced to forty years; Glenn got twenty. Turman, who was only sixteen at the time of his arrest, got eight years but was released in 1948. Two years later, Turman and Utah Wilson would gain even greater notoriety.

6

TOUGH TOWN

The Murder of Captain Frank Tatum

War is safer than standing on a Portland street.
—*William Kilpock*

While Utah Wilson was on the run from the Washington State Reform School and his older brothers served time in the Oregon State Penitentiary in Salem, Portland was undergoing social changes at a rate it had never seen before. Mass transit and environmental quality suffered as Detroit began to manufacture cars again, and gasoline and tires became more accessible. Wealthier Portlanders bought the new cars that were rolling off the assembly lines in the place of tanks, bombers and liberty ships and sold their old junkers to used car dealers. These businesses sprang up like mushrooms along Eighty-second Avenue and in the traditional "auto row" near the east end of the Burnside Bridge. Cheap used cars gave a new freedom of movement to the working class and the young. Drive-in movies and restaurants flourished, and pioneering teenagers began to cruise "the Loop" along Southwest Broadway and Sixth Avenue. Broadway, lined with movie and variety theaters and their distinctive neon signs, was the entertainment capital of the region. People from rural communities all over southwest Washington and up the Columbia and Willamette Rivers made their way to Portland on a regular basis for shopping and to "go to the show."

And what a show it was. First-run movies dominated the Broadway strip at the Paramount, Orpheum and J.J. Parker's Broadway and Music Box, as well as many others. A few blocks off Broadway, Sam Herman's Clover Club or Al Winter's Pago Pago Room provided upscale dining, drinking and entertainment. Farther off Broadway, the Will Mastin Trio, featuring twenty-year-old "Sunshine Sammy" Davis Jr., regularly played the Capitol Theater, which hadn't gone burlesque yet. For those with wilder tastes, Northeast Broadway offered the Dude Ranch, providing the exciting new "race" music rhythm and blues, which was transforming American music. At the Dude Ranch, Jack McVea, "the leader of just another Negro orchestra," was performing his novelty song that immortalized the crowded living conditions along Williams Avenue. "Open the Door, Richard" wouldn't be recorded until October, and then just as a joke, but it would become the first hit song from Portland, catapulting McVea from a run-of-the-mill $750 per week act to a headliner commanding $2,000 per week. Before the end of 1946, the Dude Ranch ran into

trouble with the city because of its integrated audiences. The nightclub lost its lease and closed. Another Dude Ranch, just a shadow of what it had been, opened on Northeast Union Avenue (now Martin Luther King Jr. Boulevard). Williams Avenue, the heart of "Darktown," was lined with clubs that featured the greatest jazz acts, either as headliners or for late night jam sessions with integrated audiences. Duke Ellington, Count Basie and Louis Armstrong regularly played for segregated audiences at Jantzen Beach and other places, but afterward, they would hit the Dude Ranch, the Acme Club or Jackie's for a little jam. It would still be a couple of years before Lionel Hampton refused to play for a segregated audience and began the integration of Portland's mainstream music venues.

In 1946, the Portland Police Bureau hired its first black police officers since the 1890s. George (left) and Horace Duke (right) had to partner with each other because white officers refused to ride with them. Photographer unknown. *Courtesy of the Portland Police Historical Society.*

Despite segregated housing and public facilities, opportunities were beginning to open up for African Americans in Portland. Edwin "Bill" Berry and E. Shelton "Shelly" Hill, of the Portland Urban League, began intense job-readiness programs for unemployed blacks and built bridges with white employers. The work of these two dedicated "job developers" would see African Americans begin to find employment in every neighborhood and sector of Portland. Crowded conditions in "the Colored Section"—along Williams Avenue, Union Avenue and Russell Street—forced many black Portlanders to live in the crumbling temporary housing of Vanport, where the black population exceeded 25 percent. Vanport, administered by Multnomah County, hired black schoolteachers and sheriff's deputies. Martha Jordan, who started her career in Vanport, would be among the first black teachers hired by Portland Public Schools. Matt Dishman of the Multnomah County Sheriff's Department would become an important community leader. In 1946, the Portland Police Bureau hired black officers for the first time since the 1890s. Charles Duke, a Tuskegee Airman during World War II, was hired first. His brothers, Horace and George, who were also veterans, made careers out of police work. Horace and George became a regular sight around Portland. They usually had to partner together because most white officers refused to work with them.

Opportunities for women were opening up as well. The 1930s had seen women successfully enter politics with Nan Wood Honeyman's election to the state legislature in 1934 and the House of Representatives in 1936. The daughter of C.E.S. Wood, Portland's poetic radical attorney, Honeyman was a New Deal Democrat who served in the federal Office of Price Administration (OPA) during the war and ended her public career as collector of customs for the Port of Portland. Honeyman was the first female member of Congress from Oregon, but she was not the first female in the Oregon state legislature. Dorothy McCullough Lee, who lived in Portland with her oil-executive husband, served two terms in the legislature starting in 1929 and then was elected to the Oregon Senate in 1932. During the war, she resigned from the senate when Mayor Earl Riley appointed her to a vacant spot on the Portland City Council after the death of Ralph Clyde. In 1944, she was elected to the council in her own right and served as utilities commissioner. "Dauntless Dottie" gained popularity as she fought a public battle to modernize the streetcar system. On January 16, 1946, she became the city's first female mayor when she was sworn in for the day while Mayor Riley was out of town.

Women still faced discrimination and negative attitudes from family and society in general, but Rosie the Riveter and her sisters gained a huge amount of self-confidence during the war, and many of them were not willing to return to the restricted roles they had been assigned. Many women were determined to keep working when the war ended, and even more of them, who had been successful "single mothers" during the war, were not willing to accept abusive or controlling husbands when they returned. Divorce, while still not common, began to become socially acceptable as more and more marriages succumbed. Domestic violence rose, too. Some husbands refused to give up "their rights," and although the Unwritten Law was no longer a legal defense, it was an attitude that many men still held. There were several cases of returning soldiers killing their wives, including the case of Frances Grieco, a twenty-three-year-old woman who was chased from her father's house by her husband. She ran to the Idle Hour Café, just a block away, but her enraged husband followed and stabbed her to death in front of several witnesses. The most gruesome of these killings was the so-called Pandora's

Employment of women in the shipyards and in other jobs during the Second World War drastically changed the situation and the expectations of women. When the war ended, many of them were not content to return to their kitchens. Photograph by Ann Rosener. *Courtesy of the Library of Congress.*

Box Murder, in which Jim Bowden tricked his wife, Fern, into opening his booby-trapped footlocker in the basement of their Southeast Portland home. She was blown to bits by the dynamite bomb he had built.

The murders seemed to reflect a hard attitude that Portland had developed during the war. Violent crime rose rapidly as returning veterans hit the streets and found it tough to get work. "Slugging"—violent muggings that often involved severe head injuries—became a common crime, with both men and women as victims. Barfights had always been a reality in Portland, but after World War II, they took on a new viciousness and more often ended up in murder or manslaughter. Bodies in the river had been a recurring event since the first days of the city, but they became routine in the postwar years. About a dozen bodies a year turned up in the Willamette, the Columbia or along the railroad tracks. Many of them were never identified, and even if they were identified, their deaths were rarely investigated. Throughout 1946, headlines about the Torso Murder appeared, as paper-wrapped bundles of body parts were discovered in the Willamette. Four separate packages were found over several months, containing the dismembered body of a woman in her fifties. The body was never identified and the killer never found. It was an odd coincidence that Anna Schrader, the private detective who had been the police bureau's gadfly in the '20s and '30s, went missing that year. Symbolic of the tough town that Portland had become was the attack on William Kilpock during the summer of 1946. The twenty-two-year-old veteran, recently released from the service, was standing in front of the Orpheum Theater on Broadway, waiting for the next show, when an ex–mental patient named Larry Brown hit him in the head with an axe. Kilpock survived the random attack, saying, "War is safer than standing in a Portland street."

Rising crime rates caused the city to ask legendary policeman August Vollmer to investigate the police bureau in 1947. Vollmer, first police chief of Berkeley, California, had created the criminal justice program at the University of California and earned the nickname "the father of modern policing." In 1947, in his role as president of the International Association of Police Chiefs, he visited Portland and investigated the police bureau, submitting a lengthy report. Vollmer found the police officers to be extremely well educated. Chief Niles had already taken Vollmer's advice and instituted education requirements, but Vollmer found the force to be low paid and demoralized. A high percentage of officers were in poor physical condition, and many of them were time fillers, often spotted sleeping in their patrol cars during the night shift. Many officers supplemented their meager wages by accepting "smile money"—small gifts of five dollars or so—from businesses on their beats. In return, they looked the other way at the illegal slot and pinball machines, punchboards and other gambling paraphernalia available nearly everywhere. Very few officers paid for coffee or meals, either while in uniform or off duty, and many of them took on an attitude of privilege, as if they were above the law. Vollmer didn't look too hard at the graft and corruption that was prevalent in the police bureau, but his visit spurred the city club to begin an investigation of graft conditions that they would publish in 1948.

In 1946, vice was flourishing. Al Winter had a few problems with the Oregon Liquor Control Commission (OLCC), who never liked to give him or his partners a liquor license. The Turf Club suffered a few embarrassing gambling raids, but that might have been pressure from his ambitious subordinate Jim Elkins, who controlled the Vice Squad through police captain Jim Purcell and others. Elkins also brought pressure on Winter by periodically robbing his partners. Milton Hyatt and Barney Morris, both partners with Winter in the Pago Pago Room and Turf Club, were robbed at gunpoint. Hyatt was robbed at least three times. Elkins had problems of his own, though. In May 1946, someone set fire to his "after hours" club on Southwest Fifteenth Avenue, exposing the gambling operation that was carried on upstairs. Elkins's tight organization controlled a good portion of the illegal activity in town, but he still needed Winter's connection to Mayor Riley.

Elkins recruited outlaws young and old and put them to work, rewarding them with saloons or clubs to run under the supervision of Earl Bell. Nick DePinto, the leader of the old DePinto brothers gang, now an aging ex-con, ran the 318 Club for Elkins on Northwest Couch Street. Chuck Brown, an ex-boxer who worked for Elkins for years, ran a place on Northwest Third Avenue. Brown's place was just off Burnside Street, around the corner from Burke's Café and the Hotel Clare. Elkins also owned the 26 Club around the corner on Northwest Fourth Avenue. Harold "Hal" Sehorn worked as a bouncer at the 26 Club. His "wife," Shirley Higdon, a "freelance nightclub photographer," scammed unwary visitors with "badger games"—extortion by impersonating police officers—and blackmail plots. "Stormy Jean" Duncan, another young woman who specialized in "rolling" drunks—getting money from drunks in various ways—spent a lot of time in the neighborhood and showed up regularly at the 26 Club.

Pat O'Day, also known as Herb Patterson, had been a popular boxer in the early 1930s. "The Reno Slugger" fought as a light heavyweight and was

After Prohibition ended in 1933, the "speakeasy culture" translated into the new "nightclub culture." During World War II and after, a night on the town often included a visit to one or more nightclubs. Photograph by John Collier. *Courtesy of the Library of Congress.*

known to have a heavy punch but not a lot of staying power. By 1940, he was being regularly knocked out in the ring and gave up boxing as a sport. By then, he had become an enforcer for Elkins's mob and continued to beat people up for a living. In 1946, he had at least ten arrests for assault and had become a little bit of a liability for Elkins. As manager of the 828 Club on Southeast Sixth Avenue and Belmont Street, O'Day had too many fights, and his till was short too many times. In September 1946, Elkins and his partner, Earl Bell, closed the 828 Club and gave O'Day one more chance at the Cecil Rooms downtown. Hal Sehorn went to work for O'Day and was told to keep the ex-boxer under control. It was an impossible job, though. Hitting people was a habit that O'Day did not want to break.

The Cecil Rooms were located on Southwest Sixth Avenue in the heart of downtown Portland. Patrons had to climb a flight of stairs and ring the buzzer to gain admittance to the two-story brick building. The door was kept locked, and the guests were viewed through a small window before being allowed entrance. The after-hours club employed a series of "runners" who spread the word about where someone could "get a drink." Also known as the 212 Club, the large room featured a bar, a jukebox, pinball, a piano and several tables surrounding a small dance floor. An adjoining room featured a large dice table. The kitchen was used by employees and only a select few guests. The Cecil Rooms didn't sell food and didn't have a liquor license. Upstairs were three rooms, one used by Pat O'Day and the others kept for favored guests and employees. O'Day's room was sometimes used for assignations by the prostitutes who often frequented the club. In January 1947, two men lived in the rooms above the Cecil Club: Johnny Snyder, a young boxer who used the name Bobby Clark in the ring, and Jimmy Barr, who sang in the club and helped Johnny train. Pat O'Day often slept upstairs, although he had an apartment on Southwest Vista Drive. O'Day spent most of his time at the club, which served illegal alcohol nearly twenty-four hours a day.

The "bootleg" clubs drew clients from all classes and occupations. Steered by "runners" from the upscale nightclubs—or taxi drivers and pimps—businessmen, middle-class couples on a night out, visitors from out of town, sailors and other transient workers looking for a drink rubbed elbows with safe-crackers, armed robbers, prostitutes and drug addicts. A regular cast of characters made the rounds of these clubs, and many of them preyed on the unwary visitors. Jimmy Barr, a bottom-of-the-barrel nightclub singer, and Lee Butler, an ex–special police officer with a record for assault who played accordion, provided the entertainment at the Cecil Rooms. Sybil Willard and her roommate, Faye Tripp, made the rounds of bootleg clubs looking for opportunities. Willard was Pat O'Day's "girlfriend," although some might have called her his punching bag. Barbara Daugherty ran the hatcheck concession and manned the door at the Cecil Rooms. Captain Frank Tatum was a frequent visitor to Portland since he captained a freight ship that made regular runs to Yokohama with grain cargos for famine-stricken Japan.

Captain Tatum had been in the Merchant Marine agency for more than twenty years and had seen a lot of action on liberty ships in the Atlantic during the war. When the war in Europe ended, he transferred to the Pacific and began to work out of Portland in 1945. In 1946, he took command of the SS *Edwin Abbey*, a former liberty ship sold by the Navy Department for civilian use. It took about six weeks to make the roundtrip to Japan with stops in Korea and mainland China. The crew would usually have about two weeks in Portland before beginning the next run. Tatum liked to have a good time during his shore leave and treated his time in Portland as a long party. He was a regular at many of the nightspots in town, especially the bootleg clubs. He had been a regular customer at the 26 Club, and he followed Hal Sehorn and his crowd to the Cecil Rooms.

On January 10, 1947, Tatum, back in Portland after a run to Japan, drew a month's pay ($615) in cash and hit the North End for a night on the town. Sometime before midnight, he turned up at the Cecil Rooms to see his old buddy, Sehorn. Tatum was having an affair with Opal Pointer, a singer at Earl Bell's Ramapo Club, and he brought a kimono for her from Japan. He checked the package with Barbara Daugherty, and he and Sehorn left for the North End to get "roaringly drunk." They ended up at Big Mike's Club on Northwest Third Avenue and Couch Street, on the same block with Nick DePinto's club and across the street from Foon Yai Yee's lottery shop. Tatum wanted to see his friends Mike and Vivian Svetic, who owned the club, but they weren't there. Instead, he and Sehorn ran into Shirley Higdon, Sehorn's partner in crime. The place was empty, except for Tatum's party, a bartender named Dave and Georgia Ramsey, who played piano.

"Let's see who can drink the other under the table," Sehorn said. Tatum was a heavy drinker when he was on shore leave, so he was up for the challenge. Tatum was also a free spender who cared little about money when he was drunk. He bought most of the drinks, piling his cash on the bar. Sehorn and Higdon helped themselves freely to the captain's money until Ramsey tried to put a stop to the looting. Tatum, well into his cups by now, told the piano player to mind her own business and waved bills around. At one point, "in a drunken stupor," he threw his wallet on the ground, strewing bills and pieces of paper across the floor. Ramsey and Higdon helped him pick up his things. Before leaving, Sehorn told Ramsey with a smirk, "I'll get all of his money if I can."

Captain Tatum lost about $400 that night, but he was not worried about it. He returned to the Cecil Club shortly after midnight on January 14. When he mentioned being "rolled," Barbara Daugherty, the hatcheck girl, sympathized. Tatum said, "Don't worry, little girl. I'll make more." The captain was his old happy-go-lucky self as he sat at the bar, buying drinks for everyone who came in. After a while, he met the Svetics and went to the Ramapo Club for dinner, taking along the kimono for Opal Pointer. Afterward, he went back to the Cecil Rooms. Pat O'Day had been in a bad

"Diamond" Jim Purcell was chief of detectives in 1947. During the investigation of Frank Tatum's murder he kept tight control of his detectives and made sure the investigation didn't turn up anything too uncomfortable for bar owner Jim Elkins. Photographer unknown. *Courtesy of the Portland City Archive A2014-004.*

mood all day; when Sybil Willard threw a tantrum at the bar because he hadn't given her a ride, O'Day knocked her to the floor twice before forcing her down into a chair. Tatum remarked, "Not much of a man who would push a woman around like that." The comment didn't sit well with O'Day. The captain spent the entire day at the bar drinking and spending heavily, until he ran out of cash at some point in the afternoon. Then things turned uglier with Pat O'Day.

Some said it was a dispute over a $100 bet. Others said it was because O'Day called Tatum a "cocksucker." Most witnesses claimed that Tatum threw the first punch, but they all lied every time they talked to the police. Whatever the beef was, O'Day spent hours beating the captain, knocking him to the floor more than once, jumping on his face with both feet and hitting him over the head with a whiskey bottle. At one point, O'Day picked up an ice pick and threatened to finish the captain, but Johnny Snyder and Hal Sehorn talked him out of it. Snyder grabbed the captain's platinum and diamond wristwatch off the floor near the jukebox and pried the onyx ring off his finger. He went through his pockets and found that Tatum still had $16 in cash. Snyder put the bills in the cash register. O'Day finally passed out, and Snyder tucked him into his bed. He and Sehorn waited until it was good and dark before carrying Tatum down to Pat's car and driving him up into the west hills. Both men said they didn't know if he was dead when they rolled him off the side of the road and down a hill overlooking what would soon be Forest Park. The truth is they didn't care.

They knew Tatum was dead for sure on Thursday when Snyder drove down Santanita Terrace and saw the body still lying where it had fallen, partially covered with snow. O'Day knew he had blown his last chance. He called a meeting of everybody who had been there on Tuesday when he had beaten the captain. He told them all that Tatum was dead and they all had to dummy up if the police asked about it. They all agreed that Tatum had been in the club until about 4:30 p.m. and then had left. On Friday, William Peterson, the steward from the *Edwin Abbey*, showed up at the Cecil Rooms looking for Tatum. The ship was scheduled to leave port on Monday, but no one had seen the captain. Peterson went to the police, and Detective Collie Stoops, an ex-boxer and popular referee, and his partner, W.L. Taylor, began an investigation. The first clue they found was a taxi driver who had seen Snyder wearing the captain's watch on Wednesday night.

The whole thing was an embarrassment for Jim Elkins, and he might have consulted with the chief of detectives, Jim Purcell. Purcell took control of the investigation, often interrogating witnesses himself and making no reports. Stoops picked up Snyder, Sehorn and O'Day right away and focused their investigation on them from the start. All of the witnesses lied when they talked to the police, each of them changing their stories at each interrogation. The detectives doggedly re-interviewed the witnesses, sometimes jailing them as material witnesses to gain their cooperation. Many of the witnesses skipped town immediately. It took Detectives Stoops and Taylor several months before they tracked down Lee Butler and Faye Tripp in Odessa, Texas. They were nervous when interviewed by FBI agents, but they kept to their story that they knew nothing about the case. Vickie Moore (real name Florence Flitcraft), a witness who heard most of the fight and was not one of the regular gang, was picked up for prostitution in Spokane several months later. She said she had been threatened and feared for her life when she left town. She was returned to Portland and became one of the main witnesses for the prosecution.

Sehorn pleaded guilty to manslaughter and eventually told the police the whole story. Snyder co-operated as well and pleaded guilty to manslaughter. O'Day was convicted of first-degree murder and sentenced to life; Sehorn and Snyder each got fifteen years. Less than twelve years later, O'Day was paroled from his life sentence and returned to Portland to finish his life drinking and bragging in Portland bars. The open-and-shut murder case was cleared up quickly, but the political fallout from the crime would not be so easily contained.

7

DOTTIE DO-GOOD TAKES CHARGE

I am not a reformer, as some persons define the word, but I believe strongly in the integrity of government…I will enforce the law.
—*Dorothy McCullough Lee*

On March 25, 1947, the Masters, Mates and Pilots (MMP) West Coast Local 90 of the AF of L ratified a resolution calling for action against the killers of MMP member Captain Frank Tatum. Calling Portland "one of the most dangerous ports for any seafaring man to go ashore in," the resolution charged that "man's life and property is in danger and organized thuggery has taken over certain sections of the city." Two days later, August Vollmer, "the father of modern policing," arrived for his inspection of the Portland Police Bureau. His report wouldn't be released until January 1948, just in time to be a major issue in the city election. The MMP and its secretary-treasurer, William O. Fischer, were not the only ones in Portland who thought that crime had gotten out of hand. A citizen's committee of ministers from local churches sent a letter to Mayor Riley, charging that Portland had become lawless and overwhelmed with "commercialized and syndicated gambling, prostitution, slot machine leasing and operation." Riley laughed off the ministers' letter as "gossip," but he was running scared.

He had been for a while—at least since the brutal murder of Foon Yai Yee in a storefront lottery shop on Northwest Couch Street, just across the street from Nick DePinto's 318 Club. Yee sold lottery tickets in the old-fashioned, hand-painted Chinatown style and conducted drawings three times a week. His

Dorothy McCullough Lee, the city's first female mayor, took office with a great deal of hope and enthusiasm and a promise to "enforce all of the laws." By the time she left office in 1952, she had sent her children out of state and carried a gun to protect herself from death threats. Photographer unknown. *Courtesy of the Portland City Archive A2011-004.82.*

locked-door shop was cluttered with junk of all kinds, including several slot and pinball machines. Yee sold a lottery ticket to Charles Berke on Christmas Day 1946, shortly before the Vice Squad raided his shop and picked up twenty-five men on gambling and "behind locked doors" charges. The Christmas Day raid was part of Captain James Purcell's public relations campaign for Mayor Riley. Purcell had recently taken command of the Vice Squad along with his duties as chief of detectives and head of the Homicide Squad. He and inspector James Fleming had divided the chief's duties between them as Leon Jenkins's health failed. The former chief had come out of retirement when Harry Niles had stepped down shortly before he died. Jenkins, nearing eighty years old, was not physically up to the job of chief, and his subordinates filled the vacuum.

The raid on Yee's lottery shop created bad blood between him and Charles Berke. Berke, a Latvian-born itinerant laborer, returned to Yee's shop on the Saturday morning after Christmas and attempted to cash a "winning" ticket for $17.50. Yee refused to pay off. At this late date, it is impossible to tell the truth of the matter, but there were two old scams involving Chinese lottery that could have been involved. Lottery is probably the oldest form of Chinese gambling in Portland and began in 1851, when Tong Sung opened his restaurant and boardinghouse on Southwest Second Avenue. The first lottery scam was probably attempted shortly after the first drawing. One scam was to forge or "raise" a winning ticket and pass it off on unwary lottery operators. The other scam worked best on non-Chinese speakers. A lottery operator would sometimes claim that a winning ticket was a forgery although it was real. The scams had gone both ways countless times and sometimes ended up with a shooting. Berke didn't have a gun, though. What he had was a heavy piece of pipe wrapped in cloth and a five-inch-long horse-blanket safety pin. He beat the Chinese lottery man severely with the homemade sap, spattering blood all around the shop. But it was two stabs to Yee's heart with the safety pin that killed him. Police got an anonymous call to a nonexistent address next door to Yee's shop. Responding officers noticed the blood inside the closed shop and broke down the door, catching Berke with the bloody murder weapons in his pocket.

The violent Saturday kicked off a brutal week that included several robberies, climaxing on Friday night with five armed robberies committed within blocks of one another. The "postwar crime wave" that J. Edgar Hoover of the FBI had been warning the nation about had come home with a vengeance. Saturday morning, one week after Yee's murder, Chief Jenkins announced "emergency measures": police would begin working twelve-hour staggered shifts to provide increased coverage; the 150-member police auxiliary was called out; and "shotgun" squads would be deployed in strategic areas when "suspicious vehicles" were spotted. Captain Purcell took responsibility for the city's three thousand ex-convicts, picking them up on "suspicion" and intimidating them into following the law or getting out of town. Many of the city's ex-convicts were safely ensconced in Jim Elkins's organization, though, and protected from Purcell. Some of Elkins's employees, such as Pat O'Day were among the worst of them but were protected as long as they kept a "low profile."

Pat O'Day didn't keep a low profile, though, and soon the Tatum murder became the rallying cry for one of Portland's periodic reform movements. Riley left town on a long "working vacation" and tasked Inspector Fleming and Captain Purcell with the thankless job of "closing down all the gambling joints in town." When Riley returned, he named Fleming the new chief of police to replace the now-hospitalized Jenkins. He praised Fleming highly for accomplishing his goal quickly and assured Portlanders that all gambling had been shut down. That probably got a good laugh at Elkins's joints. With the exception of the Cecil Rooms, Elkins's operation continued to operate with impunity. Riley was walking an unsteady tightrope as he tried to clean up the city without stopping the flow of cash from "the payoff." According to Dorothy McCullough Lee, who was still contemplating her opposition to Riley in the upcoming election, Riley was handling about $60,000 per month. As Lee said, "The mayor got the loaf and a couple of councilmen got the crumbs."

Gambling went hand-in-hand with two other vice businesses: narcotics and prostitution. Heroin and other opiates flowed into Portland from Seattle and San Francisco. The Chicago Syndicate controlled drugs on the West Coast; it was led by the heirs of Al Capone. In a few years, when the old-time mobster Waxey Gordon was released from Alcatraz, he was given control of the West Coast heroin trade as part of his "retirement package." Chicago might have had control of drugs on the West Coast, but in Portland, it was under the thumb of "Big Jim" Elkins. Criminals and ex-cons of all kinds were drawn to Portland for the wide-open entertainment scene and "the fix"—protection from the police. Eddie Cummings, an ex-convict from Texas, was no stranger to Portland. He was involved in the robbery of a southeast Portland Safeway store in August 1948 and spent several months traveling back and forth between Portland and Seattle. In October, he hit on a new scheme. Realizing that there was a good market for heroin in Portland, he began to import small packages to the River City.

Seattle was one of the West Coast cities colonized by the New Orleans mob in the 1920s and had several established Mafia families. In the late 1940s, that meant a steady supply of heroin. Cummings was able to turn a nice profit when he unloaded his first shipment of heroin to Stanley Tomachek, a Portland drug dealer. Cummings called an old friend, Edward Iacopetti, described by the *Oregonian* as a "Seattle gunman," and asked him to bring more of the white powder to Portland. Iacopetti arrived on October 7, 1948, and he and Cummings met with Tomachek to unload his narcotics. To celebrate the deal, the two men and a party of friends spent a wild evening at Al Winter's Mecca Club (now McMennamin's Crystal Hotel) and, after a drunken drive through downtown Portland, ended up at the Caples Hotel at about 2:30 a.m. Cummings, who was registered at the hotel as Mr. Duvall, and his "wife" went to their room, but before long, Cummings and Iacopetti were arguing. They argued over the split of the drug money, and possibly over a woman, before Cummings shot Iacopetti twice. Cummings went to the desk clerk and said, "I just shot a guy. I hope he's dead."

The gangland killing drew little attention, as that kind of activity had come to be expected during the reign of Mayor Riley. The judgment of historian E. Kimbark MacColl was: "Few periods in Portland history have witnessed as corrupt, morally insensitive and generally impotent a mayorship as Earl Riley's." However, at the time of the Iacopetti shooting, Riley was in the process of creating his most important legacy as mayor of Portland: Forest Park, which was formally dedicated on September 25. Riley was still running for reelection when he was approached by the citizen-run Committee of Fifty with the idea to create a large "forest park" in the west hills of Portland. It was not until he had been unceremoniously dumped from office during the May primary election, but with a term that didn't end until January 1949, that he took the lead on the project. He put together a

The devastating Vanport flood hit Portland after the election of Dorothy McCullough Lee but before she took office as mayor. The destruction of the city left thousands homeless, and the mayor faced serious social problems as Vanport's African Americans tried to assimilate into Portland. Photographer unknown. *Courtesy of the Portland City Archive A2001-083.*

deal that acquired 2,500 acres of land, foreclosed on by the city and county for tax delinquency, along with several donations of land, bringing the total to about 4,500 acres. Forest Park, opened shortly before Riley left office, was the largest park within any United States city and became a lovely forest reserve that connects to more than fifty miles of walking trails. Riley believed and hoped that he would be remembered for Forest Park, but most Portlanders don't remember his role in establishing the park.

After the Vollmer Report and the City Club Report on Policing came out early in 1948, opposition to Riley began to coalesce around the issues of crime and vice. Dorothy McCullough Lee came forward as the movement's leader. In March 1948, she announced her candidacy for mayor in the upcoming May primary. Although she faced gender discrimination, she soon became the front runner in the election. Lee's supporters were no less discriminatory than her opponents; for example, the *Oregon Journal* endorsed her "since no qualified man has stepped forward" and urged its readers to "vote for the little woman." She ended up with more than 70 percent of the vote in the primary election—the largest vote majority in any Portland election. Her victory in May meant she wouldn't have to stand for election in November, giving her nearly a year to prepare for her term as mayor. Her margin of victory left Lee feeling triumphant, as if the people of Portland were behind her. It wouldn't be long before she realized her mistake.

Beyond city hall, gender discrimination might be responsible for the silence that surrounded the subject of prostitution. Prostitution had been an accepted fact of life in Portland for more than one hundred years, but under the Elkins-Winter syndicate, it had become an efficient and vicious business. Brothels, often organized as rooming houses or hotels, were located all around Portland, usually in proximity to a bootleg club. A network of procurers and pimps captured women, often as young as fifteen, and seduced or forced them into "the life." Young women were often moved from city to city, in a network of brothels that included stops in The Dalles, Spokane, Tacoma, Seattle, San Francisco and Reno. Drug addiction, blackmail and violence were used to keep the women under control and to force them to turn their earnings over to pimps or "boardinghouse managers." Day-to-day operations and dirty work were handled by madams, such as Helen Smalley, Honey LaTourelle or Maudell Ward Lindsey, or by pimps, such as Jess Russell, who worked as a cabbie. Profits went to men who ran "respectable" businesses, often men who were very prominent and influential.

One of these brothels was located on North Mississippi Avenue, a short walk from the Opportunity Tavern on North Vancouver Street. The Opportunity was owned by Paul Ail, who had started out selling peanuts and popcorn at Vaughn Street Stadium and was well on his way to becoming the "Concessions King" who would create Portland International Raceway and buy the Portland Beavers baseball team. Ail wasn't always involved in operating the tavern, but he spent a lot of time there, and he had several friends among the Duncan family, who made the Opportunity Tavern the headquarters for their criminal activities. The thirteen children of Charles and Mary Duncan— who fled southern Missouri to escape the Dust Bowl and raised their children on relief and welfare money—were involved in all kinds of crime, but they managed to keep an extremely low profile because Paul Ail was their "fix." Ail was close to Annie Duncan, who worked as a prostitute in a northeast Portland brothel, and her brother Eddie, a United States Army deserter who directed his brothers in criminal activity similar to that of the Wilson brothers across the river. Another sister, Stormy Jean Duncan, specialized in "rolling" drunks around Burnside Street. The eldest brother, Frank Duncan, usually held a steady job, and another brother, Larry, was a member of the Teamsters' Union. Whenever there was legal trouble, Ail would pay for the defense, usually hiring Irvin Goodman, Portland's most famous and radical defense attorney. Somehow, Ail managed to avoid publicity. When Eddie Duncan was arrested as an army deserter in 1947, Ail paid his bail; the story never even made the papers.

The months between Dorothy Lee's electoral victory and the beginning of her term were a time of preparation for Portland organized crime figures. A virtual reign of terror ruled the waterfront, and several murders occurred, usually targeting members or officials of waterfront unions. One of them displayed elements of a modus operandi that would become all too familiar and would point to the Duncan gang. On July 24, 1948, William O. Fischer, secretary-treasurer of the Masters, Mates and Pilots (MMP) union, left Portland to drive to Umatilla on business. Fischer had been involved in the International Longshore Association (ILA) during the Big Strike and had been a defendant in the James Conner murder case. After the ILA broke up, Fischer moved over to the National Maritime Union (NMU) before moving into leadership in the MMP union. Fischer had consistently been a strong voice against the gangsterism that was infecting unions along the waterfront. All of the elements that would be involved in the murders in which the Duncans were found to be involved were there in Fischer's murder: abduction, a long drive on lonely rural Washington roads, a body hidden in the brush, shoes thrown from a car and multiple cars used in the escape. Two young men, Harold "Speed" Coe and Donald Lillard, both AWOL sailors, were arrested the same day the body was found. Circumstantial evidence connected the men to the crime, and they were both convicted, serving short prison terms. Coe, from Camas, Washington, had spent two years in the Washington State Reform School at Chehalis. For part of the time, he was with Utah Wilson, who lived near to where Coe grew up. After less than a decade in prison for murder, Coe moved to Portland and became a respectable businessman, founder of a successful towing company.

Just days after Dorothy McCullough Lee's victory at the polls, Paul Ail's GoKart Concession at Jantzen Beach was destroyed in the flood that washed away Vanport City. The hastily built, temporary structures of the housing project were hit by a wave nearly fifty feet high when the railroad dike along North Denver Avenue gave way, and the flooding Columbia River rushed through the gap. Residents had been assured that morning that they had nothing to worry about. They got between ten and forty minutes' warning, depending on how close they lived to the dike. Pandemonium ensued as people rushed to flee the fast-moving water that flipped cars over and knocked houses off of their foundations. Several people died, and more than 100,000, 1 in 4 of them black, were left homeless. The water continued to rise, and soon, parts of the Steel Bridge were submerged. A fifteen-pound sturgeon was caught in the waters of Union Station. The seawall, built along the river in the 1920s, held, and downtown was safe. But the financially strapped city had a huge cleanup in store and a lot of homeless people to shelter.

Paul Ail, always known for his generous contributions to charity, took the lead in opening private homes to homeless Vanporters. Many white Portland families took in homeless African American families, and often, these situations led to strong relationships. A lot of the people who took in homeless Vanporters became strong supporters of the civil rights movement, which was just getting started. Although Dorothy McCullough Lee was a conservative Republican, she was a strong supporter of civil rights and tried to pass a Public Accommodations Law, which barred segregation in public places. Like most of her measures, though, the Public Accommodations Bill died in the city council. Lee, who had won the greatest plurality of votes in Portland history, had lost most of her public support by the time she took office in January 1949.

It was partly her fault. She came into office like a bull in a china shop, reorganizing city council assignments, demoting Chief Fleming to head of the night relief and bringing Charles Pray, the man who set up the Oregon State Police in 1931, out of retirement to run the bureau. She had become convinced that enforcing the gambling laws at the lowest level—slot machines, punchboards and pinball machines—was the way to break the rackets. She enforced those laws across the board in taverns and in private clubs, such as the Portland Press Club and the Multnomah Athletic Club, which depended on their slot machines for income. And she often acted on her prejudices. In March 1950, she admonished brothers Paul and Leonard Schneiderman, owners of the Music Hall cabaret, that if they wanted to keep their license, "men who act like unladylike ladies" must not be allowed to perform. "These people have been run out of San Francisco," the mayor said. "They have got to get out of Portland, along with the undesirable persons they attract."

It wasn't all Mayor Lee's fault, though. Her campaigns against slot and pinball machines were a declaration of war against Jim Elkins. He began his planning as soon as he knew that he would have to deal with Mayor Lee. He backed a candidate for Multnomah County sheriff, Mike Elliott, who could be used against her, and he began a propaganda campaign of ridicule against the female mayor. E. Kimbark MacColl claims that Elkins received money from the Chicago Syndicate to finance his campaigns against the mayor. Wherever the money came from, the campaigns were successful. Mike Elliott was a self-destructive buffoon who lied about his education and military service and got elected sheriff with backing from Elkins, Stan Terry and other gambling interests. Part of their plan was to continue to run gambling outside Portland city limits if things got tough.

Mike Elliott was a loose cannon who could do a lot of damage to Mayor Lee if he was properly handled. Elliott, described as a "two-hundred-pound extrovert," immediately identified himself with Dorothy Lee's reform movement, vowing a "Dual Drive Against Vice." He made several spectacular raids on gambling operations in competition with Elkins and Terry. Then the truth came out about the lies on his resume. He had been dishonorably discharged from the Marine Corps, and he had never attended college at all. That wasn't enough, though. Next, he was discovered drunk with prostitutes in a Reno hotel room paid for by Jim Elkins. The resulting recall election was a disaster for Mayor Lee and fatal to the reform movement that had elected her. Portland Fire Department captain Terry Schrunk was appointed sheriff to fill the vacancy, beginning his long and brilliant political career. Schrunk was always happy to participate in the "payoff" and had no problem doing business with Elkins and his organization.

Police chief Charles Pray was in a pickle. He had come out of retirement to help his friend Mayor Lee sort the "good eggs" from the "bad eggs" in the police bureau. An outsider, he wasn't trusted by anybody in the department, which was now factionalized between Purcell and Fleming supporters. The police union had its first major victory in the November 1948 election, when the voters approved an initiative to create a "pay-as-you-go" pension fund for police and firefighters.

Donald McNamara was one of the "good eggs" handpicked by Charles Pray to succeed him as chief of police. Photographer unknown. *Courtesy of Portland Police Historical Society.*

It was the beginning of a pension system for public employees. The victory did little for the morale of the bureau, though; it seemed too little too late. Pray was excluded from information about the operation of the bureau and crime. He was especially frustrated with not being able to find out, or control, what the Vice Squad was doing. After two frustrating years, Pray had been able to identify some of the "good eggs" in the bureau who might point to a better future—officers such as Frank Springer and Donald McNamara. In 1951, McNamara stepped into the chief's office, and Pray went back to raising roses at his Eastmoreland home.

Soon, wherever Dorothy Lee went, people were making fun of her hats. The media called her "Dottie-Do-Good" and "No Sin Lee." She was even booed at Vaughn Stadium when her son threw out the first ball of the Beavers' season. Threats were made against her children, prompting the mayor and her husband to send them to boarding school in Canada for their safety. Her husband, Scotty Lee, a Standard Oil executive, unwrapped a package addressed to the mayor, which contained a dead fish wired to an alarm clock. Soon, Mayor Lee began to carry a pistol everywhere and kept it close by when she was at home.

Fear was pervasive in Portland. It was especially strong in the skid road district along Burnside Street. It was in this neighborhood that sixteen-year-old Jo Ann Dewey was starting to spend a lot of time in Portland. She was a frequent visitor to Burke's Café, where her sister's husband, Johnny Revisch, worked as a cook. Revisch would usually give Dewey a ride home to Battle Ground, Washington, when he was off, but she often had to wait awhile. She met some interesting people there, such as Stormy Jean Duncan, Joan Crawford and Roman Podlas. She heard a lot of things she shouldn't have, too, such as what happened to "the old man."

8

FORGOTTEN IN TIME

THE MURDERS OF PIERRE SCHULTZE AND ROMAN PODLAS

"There is no such thing as a perfect crime." This oft-repeated phrase is erroneous; that is, from a practical point of view.
—Rolla Crick

Unsolved murder cases in Portland were nothing new by 1948. Among the earliest (but certainly not the first) was the murder of Emma Merlotin, slain by intruders in her cottage at Southwest Third Avenue and Yamhill Street sometime during the night of December 22, 1885. Her killers were never identified, and the case remains unsolved to this day.

In the early twentieth century, there were a handful of notable cases. The year 1911 saw the murder of five-year-old Barbara Holtzman, who was lured into a Russell Street lodging house, attacked and killed by an unidentified middle-aged man. In 1924, fifteen-year-old Martha Gratke was alone washing dishes in the kitchen when an "apish creature of medium size, with long hair and dressed in a faded light suit," entered her South Portland home through the back door. After smashing her head with a stove poker, the attacker choked and gagged his victim before stabbing her through the heart. Although neighbors provided a vivid description, the identity of the violent perpetrator was never known.

In 1933 alone, there were no fewer than three unsolved homicides, including Mary Brown Strong, Virgil Maheur and W. Frank Akin. Strong, the thirty-five-year-old wife of a Reed College chemistry professor, was found dead in the bathtub of their Eastside residence. While the husband was suspected, no one was ever charged with the murder. Maheur, age

Looking east on Burnside Street at Third Avenue, this neighborhood was full of cafés, taverns and union halls frequented by seamen and other waterfront workers. Between the billboards is Burke's Café. Photographer unknown. *Courtesy of the Blendl Collection.*

thirty-four, was at a "drinking party" with friends when an argument broke out. In a huff, Maheur walked out of the room, threatening to shoot himself, but police never determined conclusively whether his ensuing death was a suicide or a murder. Akin (whose story demands a book of its own) was appointed by Governor Julius Meier to investigate the Port of Portland. Preparing to release findings about alleged irregularities in the functioning of the port commission, he was shot to death in his apartment. Former chauffeur Jack Justice was pinned for the murder and served time, but the individuals who ordered the killing and the motivation behind it were never revealed.

Nearly a decade later, in March 1942, Gwen Margaret Ponssen was found garroted in her Southeast Madison Street apartment. The thirty-five-year-old stenographer had brought two men home the previous evening from a nearby tavern for a "drinking party," and according to a neighboring tenant, the guests departed at about 2:00 a.m. Later, autopsy reports would determine that this was about four hours prior to the time of death. Although there were several suspects, the case remains open.

Another notorious case from this period was the so-called Willamette River Torso Murder. For several months in 1946, paper-wrapped parts of a decomposed body were found at several locations along the Willamette River in Portland. They belonged to a woman, about fifty years old, whose head had been fractured by a blunt instrument. The story appeared in the concluding paragraphs of Rolla Crick's Sunday, April 4, 1948 *Oregon Journal* article, "File Unsolved." Chronicling about a dozen unsolved violent crimes in Oregon and southern Washington over the previous half century, Crick called the torso case "Portland's most grisly mystery in connection with the finding of an unidentified body." Little did he know that within a week, two more bodies would be discovered in Portland that would apparently leave investigators baffled until the cases eventually faded entirely from the city's memory.

The first body was discovered on Saturday, April 10, 1948, floating in a shallow creek on Northeast 138th Avenue between Sandy Boulevard and Marine Drive. It quickly became apparent from the state of the body

The mysterious Pierre Schultze was often referred to as the "old man." The discovery of his body in the Columbia Slough was not mentioned in the *Oregonian* until three years after his death. Photographer unknown. *Courtesy of the Walter Graven Estate.*

that the man had been dead for some time. The coroner listed the death as "probably caused by asphyxiation due to drowning." Investigators eventually learned that this was forty-seven-year-old Pierre Alfred Schultze, who had come to the United States from Germany and was naturalized in 1944. He had been staying at the Portland YMCA, but little else was known with certainty at the time.

The second discovery came one day later, when Max Sherk, a hitchhiker on his way back to Astoria, noticed two bright red objects that looked like a pair of small flags in the bushes just off the road from where he was

Roman Podlas was a student at Vanport College and a merchant seaman in 1948. He was trying to get out of town when he disappeared in April of that year, just days after his "old shipmate" Pierre Schultze disappeared. Photographer unknown. *Courtesy of the Walter Graven Estate.*

standing on Germantown Road between St. Helens Road and Skyline Boulevard. On closer inspection, the flags proved to be socks. The body was in a crumpled position, facing headfirst down the steep hillside, and the shoeless feet were visible from the road a few feet above. When authorities inspected the body, they noticed several details. First, there were no personal effects such as a wallet or watch. Second, a laundry marking on the man's trousers read, "Podlas," but it was not initially clear whether this was his name or some kind of abbreviation. Third, the body had been garroted, an "angry red line" etched across his neck. Within a day, the victim would be identified as twenty-nine-year-old former Vanport College student and merchant seaman Roman Marion Podlas.

Over the ensuing weeks, the story of Podlas's death and the subsequent investigation was consistently covered in the Portland newspapers. Perplexingly, Schultze was never mentioned, even though his body had been found just one day before Podlas's.

It was not until April 1951 that Schultze's name would be mentioned in the papers. On the fifteenth of that month, a story in the *Oregonian* appeared titled "3-Year-Old Death Mystery Draws Scrutiny of Sheriff." The article described how sheriff and future Portland mayor Terry Schrunk was "reexamining the circumstances surrounding the death of Peter [*sic*] Alfred Schultze" after being "spurred on by persistent reports of an attempted 'hush-up job.'" After mentioning the date, location and manner of death of the Schultze murder, the article stated the following:

Interest in the strangulation murder of Roman Marion Podlas, a 29-year-old ex-Vanport college student and merchant seaman, whose body was found the day after Schultze's in a ditch along NW Germantown road, all but blanked out publicity concerning the death of Schultze.

While no evidence of any such publicity in newspapers, police reports or other venues has been identified to date, the article went on to describe an investigation by city and county police that was "one of the most extensive on record."

In his "re-examination" of the Schultze case, Schrunk had apparently become convinced that the victim met with an "undoubtedly…violent death" indicated by "peculiar marks along the dead man's neck leading up to one ear," revealing that Schultze, like Podlas, had been garroted. Furthermore, the sheriff learned from Multnomah County investigators that their efforts to pin down the case "did not materialize." This led to rumors that unidentified higher-ups had "called off officers and had them accept the 'dead body' report."

What county detectives had learned, according to the 1951 article, was that Schultze had been staying at the Portland YMCA until March 18, 1948. At that time, he had warned the attendant at the front desk "not to route any calls from a 'friend' to his room." This "friend" was apparently a "sexual deviate" and "a top suspect in the case in its preliminary stages." Without specifying further details, including names, the *Oregonian* article concluded confidently that Sheriff Schrunk would "conference soon" with officers and others involved to "clarify" the case. Meanwhile, the Roman Podlas case remained unsolved, despite significant attention from law enforcement and the press.

At the time of the Podlas murder, nearly 150 individuals had been interviewed by police in the hopes of shedding light on the circumstances of his death. John Jenkins, a math instructor at Vanport College, described how his former pupil had sailed to South America with the merchant marines in the summer of 1947. On his return, he had decided not to enroll in classes, opting instead to sail again in hopes of saving up for future study on the GI Bill. Jenkins and Podlas had shared a fondness for Thoroughbred horseracing, and Podlas had apparently visited Jenkins on campus not long before his death to describe the fabulous horses that he had encountered on his voyage to South America the previous summer.

Another associate was Henry Charles Wink, who had shared an apartment with Podlas in Vanport until several weeks before the latter turned up dead.

Wink was from Chicago and had recently moved to Seattle to be with a girl whom he intended to marry while completing studies at the University of Washington. Podlas and Wink had frequently played bridge with friends in neighboring apartments, but these friends also told investigators that Podlas spent most of his time alone and did not seek out a new apartment mate after Wink left. Furthermore, they mentioned that on March 3, 1948, Podlas was paid a visit by "'an old shipmate he had met on a trip as a merchant sailor." While this detail was included in the *Oregon Journal* without specifying who this "old shipmate" was, the investigation found that Roman Podlas knew Pierre Schultze and that Schultze had been working as a ship detective (or pretending to be one).

Along with vague but enticing reports from Podlas's associates, the timeline of Podlas's final days was shrouded in mystery. It was established that Podlas was last seen at his Vanport apartment on the night of Tuesday, April 6, and left early the next morning after tidying up the place and neatly folding his pajamas underneath his pillow. Other witnesses initially reported seeing Podlas as late as Friday, April 9. These were employees and frequenters of several cafés in the vicinity of Third Avenue and West Burnside Street in Portland. According to witnesses, Podlas had been coming to these cafés for several months, spending his time there and at the nearby maritime union hall.

One waitress recalled speaking with Podlas about 7:30 a.m. on Thursday, April 8, and several others stated that he was in the café writing a letter to his sister, Clara Cwiklinski (who was later determined to be his sole living kin), back home in South Bend, Indiana, that afternoon. A merchant sailor named Raymond Moody, who had shipped with Podlas and "knew him well," told police how he encountered Podlas with a young blond woman at the corner of Second Avenue and Madison Street at about 4:00 p.m. that Friday. Podlas introduced the woman as "Barbara" and gave a French-sounding last name that Moody could not recall. Moody went on to describe how Podlas seemed worried and nervous. When asked what was wrong, Podlas replied, "A fellow is looking for me," and added that he was afraid "we'll have a beef." Moody asked who the man was, but Podlas declined to answer and said he would "take care of it himself." The *Oregonian* article goes on to state that Moody "told police Podlas intimated he'd had trouble with the man before"—suggesting that Moody did know the man's identity. Police were subsequently informed that Podlas had had trouble with a man over a ten-dollar loan the previous month.

Another witness came forward to report that a large, dark blue or green automobile with its engine running and headlights on was seen at about 2:00

In the days before Roman Podlas disappeared, he was spending much of his time at the Sailors' Union office at Southwest First and Burnside Streets. When he wasn't trying to get a ship assignment, he was often at Burke's Café, two blocks west. Photographer unknown. *Courtesy of the Oregon Historical Society #bb011919.*

a.m. on Sunday, April 11, just down Germantown Road from where Podlas's body would be discovered later that day. At the car's location, police found a green metal shipyard helmet.

While the witness reports initially suggested a straightforward chronology of events leading to the discovery of the body "dead approximately 36 hours" on Sunday, April 11, a significant wrinkle in the case came to complicate that time sequence. Just three days after the body was discovered, Helen Pachkopsky came to police with a newly re-soled moccasin-type shoe that she had found on Wednesday, April 7, not far from the spot where Podlas's corpse would turn up. Authorities determined that the shoe indeed belonged to Podlas, raising the perplexing question of how it ended up on Germantown Road four days before the body.

As investigators scratched their heads over the question of the shoe, they continued to pursue the mysterious blond woman who had accompanied Podlas. They had learned that, in addition to a French-sounding last name (never printed in the papers), she walked with a slight limp and had a half-moon scar above her upper lip. While the *Oregon Journal* reported on Thursday, April 15, that police had abandoned the theory that the blonde and dark blue or green automobile were linked to the killing, an *Oregonian* article dated Thursday, April 29, 1948, presented the breaking news that the mysterious blonde had been located in Seattle and was being questioned for information about the case.

The enigmatic chronology of events introduced by the discovery of Podlas's shoe caused several witnesses to change their stories. The coroner's autopsy report, which initially said that death occurred "no more than 36 hours before" the discovery of the body, was, on April 16, revised to read that "death had occurred any time within one week" of when the body was discovered. And five café employees and patrons at the Third Avenue and West Burnside Street establishment who had reported seeing Podlas as late as Friday, April 9, all agreed that they had not actually seen him after Monday, April 5.

Even more perplexing was the question of motive in the case. Several articles mentioned that Podlas had financial troubles, but a check for $200 was among the possessions found left behind in his apartment. Whether money or another explanation was at the heart of the matter, Podlas was clearly trying to leave Portland. For a number of days prior to his murder, he had gone to the Sailors' Union of the Pacific Hall on First Avenue and West Burnside Street (site of the Portland Rescue Mission today) in hopes of gaining passage on an outgoing vessel. He had obviously not succeeded. Furthermore, witnesses tipped detectives off to the discovery of a suitcase found in the vicinity of Podlas's body before police arrived that Sunday afternoon. While efforts to locate this suitcase failed, the possibility that he was carrying one corroborates the evidence that he was in the process of getting out of town.

Clearly, Podlas was worried that someone wanted him dead. In addition to the conversation with Ralph Moody, he had talked to another friend at his apartment about how to survive a garroting attack. The technique, which had become increasingly known to Americans during World War II, where it was touted as a preferred assassination method among specialized Nazi operatives in Europe, involved asphyxiation by way of a thin rope or wire looped over the victim's head and pulled taut in one quick and silent motion. If the victim could grab the loop in time, death might be avoided. In Podlas's case, this was not a possibility since he was found with his hands bound behind him, and it appeared that he had been tortured.

The Podlas case had vanished from the Portland papers by the end of April 1948, but it would resurface in surprising ways over the next several years. When Sheriff Schrunk called for an inquiry into a possible link between the

Roman Podlas and Pierre Schultze murders in the spring of 1951, Portland city detectives Robert McKeown and Floyd Smith took up the case. A former chauffeur, Smith had been with the Portland Police Bureau since 1929 and specialized in cases involving monetary extortion. McKeown had worked in the Vancouver and Swan Island shipyards during World War II and joined the Portland police in 1943.

McKeown was the stepson of Captain William "Big Bill" Browne, and at six feet, five inches, and 280 pounds, he could have easily assumed a similar moniker. While there is no evidence that McKeown was active in the Red Squad along with his stepfather and John Keegan, newspaper reports from the Podlas investigation reveal that "Big Bill" Browne himself was the primary spokesperson for the Portland police to the press in the Podlas case. Following notice in the press that McKeown and Smith would

Robert McKeown—stepson of police captain William "Big Bill" Browne, one of the original members of the Red Squad—took charge of the investigation into the deaths of Schultze and Podlas when the case was reopened in 1951. Photographer unknown. *Courtesy of the Portland City Archive A2014-004.*

Right: Floyd Smith was a fourteen-year police bureau veteran when rookie Bob McKeown became his partner. Photographer unknown. *Courtesy of the Portland City Archive A2014-004.*

handle the reopened investigation, there was no follow-up report of their findings about possible connections between the Schultze and Podlas deaths. In fact, the record is completely silent about the renewed inquiry.

Then, in 1952, another article appeared about the possibility of a connection between Pierre Schultze and Roman Podlas. This time, there was question of whether a third murder victim was also related to these killings. This victim was Jo Ann Dewey, and her story (while not entirely forgotten to history) demands closer investigation.

9

THE "STRANGE" CASE OF
JO ANN DEWEY

Washington newspapers made quite a point of fact that we were going to investigate the case. I don't want them to attach an undue or exaggerated importance to our failure to go ahead with it.
—*Erle Stanley Gardner*

On Friday, June 30, 1950, in the Clark County courtroom in Vancouver, Washington, Judge Eugene C. Cushing Jr. sentenced brothers Turman Galilee Wilson, twenty-four, and Utah Eugene Wilson, twenty, "to be hanged [by] the neck until dead." The two had been found guilty of the kidnapping and murder of eighteen-year-old Jo Ann Dewey and would become the first pair of brothers to be executed together in Washington state history. For more than sixty years, Jo Ann Dewey's family, and most Portlanders and Vancouverites, would believe that the two young men had abducted the young woman for rape and had killed her in the process. Some questioned the young men's guilt from the start, but it would take more than a generation for the story to begin coming out that there was another motive and that others were involved as well.

A few months earlier, on March 19, 1950, Dewey had left her job as a kitchen worker at the Portland Adventist Sanitarium on Sixtieth Avenue and Southeast Belmont Street in the Mount Tabor neighborhood of Portland and was en route back to her parents' home in Battle Ground, Washington. At 10:25 p.m., she purchased a bus ticket for Vancouver at the downtown Portland depot. About an hour later, at the Vancouver Central depot, she phoned her mother, Anna Elizabeth Dewey, to request a ride home. Mrs.

Utah Wilson and his brothers were well known to the Vancouver police. At the time of Dewey's murder, Utah was on probation for an assault and battery conviction, and he had been arrested dozens of times. Photographer unknown. *Courtesy of the Washington State Archive AR129-5-8-ph023442.*

Turman Wilson, Utah's older brother, had already served two years for rape by the time he was twenty years old. He and his brothers were "usual suspects" for the Vancouver Police Department. Photographer unknown. *Courtesy of the Washington State Archive AR129-5-8-ph023441.*

Dewey replied that she would be unable to pick her daughter up that evening and suggested that Jo Ann walk about a quarter mile to St. Joseph's Hospital, where a family neighbor worked as a nurse. Dora Crull would be able to take Jo Ann home after she finished her night shift.

At approximately 11:40 p.m., residents of the Central Court Apartments and nursing students at the nearby St. Joseph's Hospital heard the terrified screams of a woman in the street. A handful of bystanders witnessed an older model dark sedan pull up alongside a young woman walking hastily along the sidewalk. Two men, one wearing a hat and another with bushy hair, jumped out of the vehicle and grabbed her. She started to protest loudly, prompting one apartment resident to shout out a complaint about the noise. In response, one of the men yelled, "Shut up! This is my wife." The woman replied, "I'm not, I'm not!" They attempted to pull her into the car, but she resisted. Grabbing onto a telephone pole guy wire, she held on so tightly that it bent. The men began to punch her in the head and face and finally succeeded in dragging her into the backseat. With headlights darkened, the car sped off into the night. Several witnesses would later testify that they were unable to read the license plate number because caked-on mud made it illegible. Vancouver police officers Carl Forsbeck and Frank Irwin were at the scene of the abduction a few minutes later; they recovered a torn plastic strap from a lady's black purse and a small hair barrette. Nearby was a stubby Olympia beer bottle partially full of sudsy beer. On the bottle were fingerprints that would later be determined to belong to Utah Wilson.

The next day, March 20, Anna Dewey phoned the Vancouver Police Department to report that her daughter had not come home the previous night and was now missing. This prompted expansive searches across the region initiated by Vancouver police chief Harry Diamond and Clark County sheriff Earl Anderson, but these came up empty. Then, on the morning of Sunday, March 26, a trio of fishermen arrived at an isolated spot on the Wind River in neighboring Skamania County near the town of Carson, Washington. Greeted by the powerful odor of carrion, they initially expected to find a poached deer carcass in the vicinity. Instead, they discovered the nude and battered body of Jo Ann Dewey lying on a gravel sandbar. When officials searched the area, they found no clothing or personal effects. The body was removed by the Clark County sheriff and examined initially by county coroner Roy Spady, who pronounced that she had been dead about a week and had suffered a massive cerebral hemorrhage. A second examination by a chief pathologist at the Oregon State Police crime lab would show that the actual cause of death was

Jo Ann Dewey graduated from the Columbia Adventist Academy in 1949. Although she was not quite eighteen, her young life had already taken a fatal turn. Photographer unknown. *Courtesy of the Columbia Adventist Academy 1950 Yearbook.*

carbon monoxide poisoning following a severe beating and apparent sexual assault.

By the time Jo Ann Dewey was buried in the Brush Prairie Cemetery near Battle Ground, Washington, on Wednesday, March 29, city police in Sacramento, California, had been notified by the FBI to be on the lookout for a used Oldsmobile that had been purchased several days prior by Turman Wilson using the alias Ted E. Davis. At 4:15 p.m. the next day, the parked vehicle was located several blocks from the governor's mansion in Sacramento. Within hours, Turman and Utah returned to the car and were promptly arrested and charged with Dewey's abduction and murder. In Utah's possession was a Llama .25-caliber semi-automatic pistol. Also found in the pocket of a jacket lying on the front seat of the vehicle was a .38-caliber six-shot revolver. Police had been tipped off about the whereabouts of the Wilson brothers by their brother Grant. The only one of five living siblings without a criminal record, Grant was characterized as the "good brother" by the press. He was a married homeowner and member of the Assembly of God Church in Camas, Washington. When questioned by police, he explained that his two brothers had fled for California because they feared the revocation of Utah's parole on account of a power saw that he had been accused of stealing from a Larch Mountain tree farm where he worked. Utah was on a two-year parole after serving a year in prison for a 1948 assault and battery conviction. Turman also had a record, having spent six years in jail for the 1942 abduction and rape of a seventeen-year-old girl (for which his brothers Rassi and Glenn were in the process of serving twenty-year jail sentences). It turned out that Turman and Utah had also stolen over $3,000 in nickels from Portland slot machines that same year. That money probably belonged to Jim Elkins, given that he controlled the slot machine racket.

"Good brother" Grant went on to explain that Turman had quit his job at the Washougal Woolen Mill on Saturday, March 18, to accompany Utah in his flight. According to Grant, the two brothers had been at his house on Monday, March 27, when they told him that they were next going to visit their father, Mose Wilson, at his trailer home in Silverton, Oregon, near the state capital. Mose himself had a solid criminal record, including serving time in the Washington State Penitentiary in 1933 for the molestation of a thirteen-year-old. He was now living apart from his estranged wife, Eunice (who lived with Turman and Utah in Camas). On Wednesday, March 29, Turman phoned Grant from a hotel in Sacramento to check on police inquiries. When Grant shared this information with police, he apparently assumed that the stolen power saw was at the heart of the matter. He also confirmed that his brothers had recently borrowed two cars registered in his name, a cream-colored Pontiac sedan abandoned in Portland and a black Buick parked in front of Grant's home in Camas.

In custody, Turman and Utah proclaimed their innocence. They echoed their brother Grant's explanation about Utah's parole violation concerns as

Earl Anderson was a political appointee as sheriff of Clark County and seen as an outsider. He hired a whole new staff of deputies, pictured here at a party in 1949, and was often at odds with Harry Diamond and the Vancouver police. Photograph by Earl Anderson. *Courtesy of the Howard Hanson Collection.*

the reason that they were hiding out in Washington and Oregon in the days after the Dewey abduction and as the reason they fled to California after that. They also made clear that on the night of March 19, they were at the Playhouse Theater on Southwest Morrison Street in downtown Portland, watching the double-billed films *Captain Caution* (1940) and *Captain Fury* (1939). According to both brothers, they were staying in Portland at the nearby Morrison Hotel with Utah's seventeen-year-old wife, Lucille. Utah and his young bride had recently married, and the two-night visit to Portland on the twentieth and twenty-first was to be their belated honeymoon. This "alibi" was undercut when Lucille testified that she saw Turman coming into the building in the middle of the night on the twenty-first, when police determined that Dewey's body had been moved to the Wind River. Waiving extradition, the brothers were brought back to Washington, accompanied by Chief Diamond and Sheriff Anderson, where they faced arraignment and were held without bail. A trial was scheduled for June 12, 1950, and Portland defense attorney Irvin Goodman and Vancouver attorney Stanford Clement were appointed as defense council. Attorney R. DeWitt Jones would prosecute the case in Judge Cushing's courtroom.

After five days of testimony from thirty-four witnesses—including an FBI fingerprint expert and Jo Ann Dewey's mother, Anna—the state rested its case on Tuesday, June 20. As he would do again in his closing argument, Prosecutor Jones honed in on the beer bottle fingerprints, the fact that the defendants switched automobiles no fewer than three times in the days following the abduction and the fact that the brothers evaded police by fleeing to California after the body had been found. In turn, the defense focused on the theater alibi, and four usherettes from the Playhouse Theater testified to having seen the defendants at the theater, although they could not specify the times and date. One insisted that she had seen them at 8:30 p.m. on the night of March 19, but the manager's work records showed that she herself was apparently not working at the theater that night (although her own work records showed otherwise). Turman and Utah also presented their own testimony, emphasizing the theater alibi along with the fear about Utah's parole being revoked as the motivation for their trips between Washington and Oregon in several vehicles before fleeing to California in the Oldsmobile.

As the trial neared a close, the defense focused on the fact that none of the state's witnesses had provided testimony or hard evidence linking Utah and Turman to the actual kidnapping and murder of Jo Ann Dewey. No one who witnessed the abduction on the night of March 19 could positively

Jo Ann Dewey worked for only a short time at the Adventist Sanitarium near Mount Tabor before she disappeared. Investigation showed that she took the job in Portland to get away from an affair with a married man. Photographer unknown. *Courtesy of the General Conference of Seventh Day Adventists Archive.*

identify the defendants as the abductors, and the entire case was based on circumstantial evidence. According to the defense, this included the beer bottle. Goodman told the court how the bottle could have been planted given that Utah lived just a few blocks from the scene of the crime and had complained about police rifling through his garbage on previous occasions. In addition, the Wilson brothers were more or less "usual suspects" in Harry Diamond's Vancouver. Diamond, who guarded his independence fiercely but still managed to co-operate with Portland authorities and operators, seemed to have a grudge against the Wilson family, arresting the boys frequently.

Despite Goodman's efforts to characterize the investigation by law enforcement as inept and the Wilson brothers as scapegoats to cover this ineptitude, the jury returned a guilty verdict, and Utah and Turman were sentenced to hang for the crime. Yet almost immediately, the defense moved for a new trial based on judicial error, and the execution date was stayed until the appeal process had run its course. Over the next two years, the case would experience a record-breaking five appeals, including the granting of an unprecedented executive stay from the governor of Washington, Arthur B. Langlie. There would be several unsuccessful petitions for Supreme Court rehearings at both the state and federal levels, and the date of execution would be revised five times before finally taking place at midnight on January 3, 1953.

Toward the end of the appeals process, while Turman and Utah awaited their impending execution at the state penitentiary in Walla Walla, Washington, Erle Stanley Gardner paid the brothers a visit. Gardner was a well-known writer who had created the Perry Mason mystery series. A self-taught attorney who passed the California state bar exam in 1911 and practiced law there until the early 1930s, he had authored over three-dozen Perry Mason novels by the early 1950s, as well as hundreds of detective stories published in pulp magazines. By the time he visited the Wilsons, he had already devoted countless hours to a project that he called the Court of Last Resort. Working in collaboration with experts in the fields of forensics, handwriting analysis, polygraph testing and other specializations, Gardner carefully reviewed criminal cases in which defendants were dealt potentially unfair sentences either because they received inadequate legal representation or because of some other miscarriage of justice (such as fabricated evidence) that prevented the individuals from a fair and thorough trial.

Decades before Barry Scheck and Peter Neufeld at the Benjamin N. Cardozo School of Law established the Innocence Project, popularizing the use of DNA analysis to reverse wrongly convicted criminals, Gardner's board of investigators successfully reversed a number of wrongful convictions through their careful analysis and research of the legal records. Perhaps most famous was the case of William Marvin Lindley, who in 1943 had been sentenced to death for the murder of thirteen-year-old Jackie Marie Hamilton alongside the Yuba River in California. By reexamining the time sequence of the murder, Gardner was able to determine that Lindley was nowhere near the scene of the crime when it happened. As a result, Governor Earl Warren commuted Lindley's sentence to life in prison, and he was later released on parole.

With a number of successful Court of Last Resort cases under his belt, Gardner arrived at Walla Walla in August 1952, prepared to consider the Wilson's case. With him were two members of his board of investigators. These included Thomas Smith, a former Washington State penitentiary warden, and Alex L. Gregory, former president of the American Academy of Scientific Investigators and one of the country's leading polygraph experts. The plan was to subject both Utah and Turman to polygraph testing in the hopes of confirming or disconfirming their involvement in the abduction of Jo Ann Dewey. The reason for doubt (and for the multiple appeals by defense attorney Goodman) stemmed from audio recordings made of the Wilson brothers conversing in their cell at the Clark County Jail back in 1950. For nearly eight months, starting in April 1950, Clark County sheriff Earl Anderson had secretly recorded the Wilsons conversing in their shared cell. Amidst some public protest, the brothers were put together into a single cell in the women's quarters of the jail with the hopes that their conversation might reveal insight into the case. The initial results of the wire recordings were somewhat inaudible, given the cavernous echoes of the space coupled with the muffled din of the hidden microphone. On careful and repeated listenings, Anderson noticed that Utah and Turman were discussing other individuals seemingly involved in the Dewey case. They were also specifying locales and vehicles. Perhaps most intriguing of all, they seemed to be referencing other homicides in relation to the Jo Ann Dewey murder.

In the fall of 1952, when the Wilsons were reaching the end of their appeal efforts, Anderson contacted Multnomah County detective Walter E.

Howard Hanson was a rookie sheriff's deputy in 1950. He was involved with wiretapping the Wilsons' cell, and he accompanied Sheriff Anderson all through the investigation. Photographer unknown. *Courtesy of the Howard Hanson Collection.*

Graven. Graven had recently been asked to assist Portland sheriff (and later mayor) Terry Schrunk in solving several homicide cold cases from 1948, and Anderson realized that their paths were now fated to cross. For a stretch of days in late September and early October, Graven, accompanied by his wife, Gerry, and police officer son, Jack, pored over the recordings in their living room. He was receiving assistance from his kin to compensate for his own hearing, which had become slightly impaired as a result of his work as a guard at the noisy Portland shipyards during the Second World War. With his younger children, Terry and Gloria, sound asleep in the neighboring rooms, Graven kept the front curtains drawn. He had already faced resistance from superiors in his efforts to investigate the cases, and on several nights while listening to the recordings, several suspicious vehicles, including a 1938 Chevrolet with headlights dimmed, had parked in front of the house before speeding off. While the recordings had been improved by the assistance of sound engineers, much of the content was still garbled and difficult to decipher. Yet as the family listened, they became more and more certain of what they were hearing. Utah and Turman were talking about their involvement in the murders of Pierre Schultze and Roman Podlas. And it was becoming clear that Jo Ann Dewey's death was directly linked to those other two deaths.

When Erle Stanley Gardner and his colleagues met with the Wilson brothers at Walla Walla just a few months before the impending executions, it was expected that they might be willing to talk on record about Podlas and Schultze. Sheriff Schrunk would soon deny that the brothers were offered a promise of clemency in the Dewey case if they admitted to involvement in the other two murders, but the newspapers printed this detail at the time. As Gardner would go on to describe in his Court of Last Resort article for *Argosy* magazine entitled "The Strange Murder of Jo Ann Dewey," Turman and Utah offered little in the way of revelatory information during their polygraph tests. In his article, though, Gardner did not mention the Podlas and Schultze cases and provided minimal details about the contents of the Wilsons' wire-recorded conversations. Along with several enticing snippets of conversation between the Wilson brothers, Gardner merely said this: "Some of those conversations are distinct. Some of them are unintelligible. Some of them are cryptic."

Even after a second round of testing with the arrival of Earl Anderson and his deputy Howard Hanson the following day, the brothers' answers to "significant" questions not specified in Gardner's article did not bear fruit. However, when asked about the involvement of a 1941 black Chevrolet sedan in the abduction of Jo Ann Dewey, Utah's response proved potentially telling. As polygraph expert Alex Gregory explained to Gardner and Anderson, "Every time when I mentioned a 1941 black Chevrolet sedan there has been a distinct and significant change in the blood pressure of Utah. That change is such as to indicate an emotional disturbance." Utah went on to admit that there was significance here, but when pressed to explain why mention of the car might elicit an "emotional disturbance," he remained silent. Without cooperation from the brothers, Gardner concluded that a full-scale investigation would be a "waste of our time and effort." Privately, he told Sheriff Anderson that Utah was "hanging himself," and he and his staff left Walla Walla to pursue other cases. For Earl Anderson and Walter Graven however, the journey to discover the truth was only beginning.

10

THE LISTENERS

I want to thank you for your confidence in me, and feel that it will not be shaken when the Podlas case is, and I feel it will be, cleared.
—Walter Graven

By the time Earl Anderson and Walter Graven were working together in 1952 to pursue connections between the murders of Pierre Schultze, Roman Podlas and Jo Ann Dewey, Anderson was no longer the sheriff of Clark County, Washington. He had lost the previous election, due largely to an incident that had taken place just a few days after the abduction of Jo Ann Dewey.

On Saturday, March 25, 1950, Sheriff Anderson had received a call to come to the home of Harold Cusic, a Washington State patrol officer in Meadowglade, Washington. As Cusic told Anderson, "There is a screwball out here" who allegedly had information about the Dewey case. Cusic had already shared information with the Clark County Sheriff's Office when Anderson and several deputies paid a visit earlier that same week on the night of Tuesday, March 21. At that point, the officer learned that Jo Ann Dewey had been having an affair with another Meadowglade resident, Donald Strawn, who was married, had three children and was a deacon in the local Seventh-day Adventist Church.

When Anderson and two deputy sheriffs arrived at the Cusic residence on Saturday evening, they found the "screwball," a church member named Colin Cree, sitting in the living room. Also present were a number of neighbors—including Grayston Crull (another deacon and the father of Jo

Earl Anderson had two years' experience as an officer of the California Narcotics Bureau before he was appointed sheriff of Clark County. His career was ruined by the Jo Ann Dewey case, but he never gave up trying to solve it. Photographer unknown. *Courtesy of the Earl Anderson Estate.*

Ann's friend Jackie Crull); his wife, Dora (who was supposed to drive Jo Ann home on Sunday night after her hospital shift); and Jo Ann's parents, Clyde and Anna Dewey. Anderson promptly asked Cree what he was doing "out here," and Cree told Anderson to speak louder because he did not have his hearing aid in. The conversation quickly became quite loud. Anderson told Cree that he was "a number one suspect" in the Jo Ann Dewey case, reassuring the others gathered in the room that Cree was currently out of jail on bail after having been served a "morals charge." As Anderson recalled later, "I also told them the information [Cree] had to offer concerned the abduction by three men of a 16-year-old girl we had recently removed from Cree's house at 2 a.m." Anderson went on to explain that the only purpose of the abduction was to threaten to kill the girl if she testified in court against Cree. At this point, Cree jumped up and prepared to strike the sheriff. The deputies seized him just as Anna Dewey came to Cree's defense, saying, "We should listen to what he has to say." Cree was removed forcibly from the house and later claimed to have suffered wounds as well as hearing loss as a result of the altercation.

Shortly after the episode at the Cusic household, Colin Cree was arrested and charged with contributing to the delinquency of a minor and also with "carnal knowledge of a minor." At his May 22, 1950 trial, which the *Oregonian* said "in no way concerns the Jo Ann Dewey case," the "girl" testified that she had "intimate relations" with Cree. He denied it, claiming that "the girl had come to his home for work he earlier had offered her." He had also written a letter to the victim's parents, requesting that charges be dropped "to protect the girl's character." He was found guilty, but the verdict was delayed after Cree vanished from court and was found hiding out at his home in Orchards, not far from Meadowglade.

Just days after his own trial, Cree filed a lawsuit against Earl Anderson and his deputies, asking for $5,000 in damages, citing bodily harm. Witnesses against Anderson, including both of Jo Ann Dewey's parents, testified that Anderson and his deputies had been drinking prior to their arrival (as the sheriff and deputies themselves admitted) and were intoxicated when they came to the Cusic home on Saturday, March 25, 1950. They further accused the sheriff and his associates of inciting violence by preemptively assaulting Colin Cree. This time, Cree was victorious. Anderson and his deputies faced severe public scrutiny as a result of the intoxication claims, and all of them were replaced after the next sheriff's election at the end of 1950. Yet Anderson's troubles with the citizens of Meadowglade and the wider Vancouver region did not stop his efforts to pursue the Jo Ann Dewey case and, later, with Detective Graven, the connections between Dewey's murder and the killings of Pierre Schultze and Roman Podlas.

The Wind River High Suspension Bridge northeast of Portland overlooked the lonely stretch of river where Jo Ann Dewey's body was dumped. Evidence suggests that the Duncans routinely threatened to throw victims from this bridge. Photographer unknown. *Courtesy of the JB Fisher Collection.*

On that previous Tuesday night, March 21, 1950, two sheriff patrol cars, along with the car of Washington State patrolman Dick Reaksacker, made their way from the small town of Washougal, Washington, up toward Meadowglade after Sheriff Anderson received a radio call to contact Jackie Crull at her home there. The route they took on several country and state roads was significant because, a few weeks later, Anderson would determine from the wire-recorded conversation between Turman and Utah that Turman and several other individuals had seen the three patrol cars pass by that night as the body of Jo Ann Dewey was being moved. Turman tells his brother on the recording, "Anderson had two cars right there…there were three cars counting Dick's." He also explains to Utah that they would have been fine leaving the body hidden in a culvert in the brush if not for "those guys and Johnny Revisch." Johnny Revisch was Jo Ann Dewey's brother-in-law, who had been married to her sister Grace and who worked as a cook at Burke's Café on Burnside Street and was staying at the Hotel Clare across the street (where owners Honey and Richard LaTourelle made sure that their customers were well provided with sex and drugs). Jo Ann had called Revisch the night of the abduction to request a ride home as she often had in the past.

On the night of March 21 and the next morning, Anderson and his colleagues met with Jackie Crull and Washington patrolman Harold Cusic. They learned about the affair with Donald Strawn and also that Jo Ann was seeing another young man from Meadowglade named Tom Gray, with whom she had quarreled the previous week. Jackie went on to explain that Jo Ann had had something important to tell her, "which no one could hear or know about," but they never had a chance to discuss it. At both meetings with the lawmen, Jackie Crull reassured the sheriff that she had no knowledge of Jo Ann's whereabouts or her fate. Later that same afternoon, Deputy Neal Jones met with a group of Meadowglade residents, including Jo Ann's parents, to discuss the question of whether to post a reward for the missing girl. Speaking alone with Jones after the meeting, Jackie Crull confided that Jo Ann had been murdered and that "a search of the brush" would reveal her body.

In the ensuing days before Jo Ann's body was discovered at Wind River on Sunday morning, March 26, Sheriff Anderson learned more about her lifestyle and personal contacts. He had already discovered that Jo Ann had recently moved to Portland and taken the job at the sanitarium in an effort to distance herself from Donald Strawn since the two had made the decision to break off the affair. From numerous friends and acquaintances, Anderson learned that Jo Ann Dewey was not "the good Christian girl"

By 1952, Burke's Café had closed its doors and Ethel's opened in its place at 309 West Burnside Street. Standing in the foreground is Officer Edward Wallo. Photograph by Allen DeLay. *Courtesy of the Portland Police Historical Society.*

that she had appeared to be. Rather, along with friends Marcia Babcock, Joan Crawford, Jackie Crull and several others, Jo Ann had been staying out into the early hours of the morning, getting picked up by young men in their cars and participating in "acts of intercourse" with them. Subsequent investigation revealed that "Jo Ann and Joan Crawford were known to most of the 'joints' on Burnside" in the vicinity of Burke's Café and the Sailors' Union of the Pacific.

Meanwhile, Jo Ann's body turned up in the Wind River, and the Wilson brothers were subsequently apprehended and eventually brought to the Clark County jail to await their trial. It was not until April 15, 1950, when the two brothers were put together in the women's section of the jail with a microphone hidden in the air ventilation system, that Anderson's own investigation started to gain real momentum. Hundreds of hours of recording were made between April 15 and June 11, when the brothers read an editorial in the *Oregonian* that mentioned Anderson and the recordings, thus tipping them off. While all of the recordings were not initially clear and decipherable, Anderson was able to determine fairly quickly that the brothers were "not innocent of the crime as they claimed." He also learned that Utah had to be told about much of the crime from his brother, suggesting that he himself had not been present. Later, Anderson and a small team of listeners, including a Clark County deputy and two Vancouver police detectives, were able to decipher other names mentioned of those who were involved. These included Marvin Colby and Len Coover.

Subsequent and lengthy investigation revealed that Colby had, until recently, been stationed in the Second Medical Battalion at Fort Lewis, Washington. Coover had been a merchant marine and was now a soldier at Fort Ord, California. Both had associations with the Sailors' Union of the Pacific hall on West Burnside Street in Portland. Tracking these two individuals led Anderson to additional individuals with helpful information. The first was Carl Johnston, another merchant marine, who told Anderson that he had loaned Coover his recently purchased maroon 1947 Ford convertible late in the night on Tuesday, March 21, 1950, after the two had been hanging out at Mom Hapham's, a Burnside District tavern popular with sailors. Johnston explained that Coover was not his usual hard-drinking self, seeming instead agitated and distant before asking Johnston if he could borrow his car. In the recordings, Turman tells Utah, "I wish we'd lost that 47 Ford with Coover and [indecipherable] in it," just before explaining how the three patrol cars passed by and almost saw them. Elsewhere, Turman asks his brother, "Didn't Leonard Coover tell you that he sent her fucking clothes flying down the chute?"

Continuing the conversation with Anderson, Johnston explained that Coover later met up with him and other sailors at an all-night Burnside District club at about 4:00 a.m., handing back the car keys and departing immediately. Johnston had not seen him since. Sheriff Anderson would go on to learn from Utah's wife, Lucille, that she had stepped out of her room at the Morrison Hotel to use the bathroom about 4:00 a.m. that Tuesday. As she was returning to the room, she saw Turman hurrying hastily back to his room across the hall in street clothes. When she asked him about this at breakfast the next morning, he said he had "slept like a log" the whole night.

The ensuing investigation of Coover led Anderson and his deputies to others with increasingly compelling connections to the crime. Under pressure, Coover had named some of the people he had met around the Burnside District in March 1950. Among others, Marvin Colby, Carl Johnston, Norm Hoover and a man named Eddie who lived out on North Interstate in Portland were mentioned. He also offered that he had met a man named "Red" Anderson at that time and that the two of them went out to dinner with two girls. "He thought their names were Marcia and Jo Ann or Joan." He had brought one of them back to his room at the Shoreline Hotel above the Sailor's Union hall. He couldn't recall which one, but the description matched Jo Ann Dewey. When asked whom he thought might have committed the crime, he said "he thought Hoover and this man named Eddie were a couple of characters and could possibly do something like this."

Eddie turned out to be Edward Duncan, one of over a dozen siblings who had settled in the Portland region when their Eastern European father had come there to work in the shipyards. When Anderson obtained a photograph of Eddie in mid-December 1950, he took it to show Laverne Akin, who lived at the Edison Hotel on Southwest Broadway. Anderson had been bringing her photographs of various individuals ever since Akin had telephoned the sheriff's office that past June to report the following story: During the week following Jo Ann Dewey's abduction, Turman and Utah came to the Roundup Theater on Southwest Morrison Street, where Akin worked in the box office. They parked their cream-colored Pontiac and waited on the sidewalk while a third man came to the window to purchase three tickets. This man was twenty to twenty-five years old; about five feet, eight inches tall; and had bushy brown hair. He was wearing clean blue jeans and a white T-shirt. What stood out to Akin was that he had deep lacerations on his knuckles and fingers that Akin said seem to have been made by teeth. Anderson had shown her pictures of Colby, Johnston, Coover and several others, but there was no match. When he brought the photograph of Eddie, she was sure that he was the man who had bought the tickets that day.

In the wire recordings, Turman tells Utah, "Larry found out that the girl was killed in his car." Anderson soon discovered that Eddie Duncan had a brother named Larry who had owned a 1941 black Chevrolet sedan around the time of the Jo Ann Dewey abduction. Several witnesses at the scene had described the abduction vehicle as either a 1941 Chevrolet or 1940/'41 Buick sedan, dark in color. It is important to note that the bodies of these two vehicles are very similar in appearance and would look nearly identical in the dark. It is also important to recall that the Wilsons often drove their brother Grant's 1941 Buick. Larry had purchased the Chevrolet on February 17, 1950, and shortly after he left town to go to San Francisco on March 22, 1950, the loan company repossessed the vehicle. When Anderson tracked it down, he found that the Chevrolet had been repainted and that the interior was covered in a "fine sand of the type used for sandblasting." At the Wilson trial, an anonymous note was passed to Utah's wife, Lucille, in the courtroom. It was brought to Judge Cushing and read, "Hi Pal Good luck. The whole gang are [sic] behind you—The man who sandblasted your shoes." Later on, when professional sound engineers worked with Anderson's recordings, a whispered conversation between Turman and Utah revealed that Eddie and Larry had indeed abducted Jo Ann Dewey in Larry's car.

Meanwhile, an ex-girlfriend of Marvin Colby's, whom Anderson discovered by way of a letter left behind at Fort Lewis, told the sheriff that she had several times visited Toledo, Oregon, with Colby, and while there, they spent time with Fred and Jean (née Duncan) Hodges, who had an apartment above the local variety store. Also there at the time were Jean's brothers Eddie and Chuck Duncan. Prior to moving to Toledo, Jean Duncan had been a well-known figure in the Burnside district of Portland. She had many nicknames, among them "Stormy Jean" Duncan. In the late 1940s, Stormy Jean had been married to a man named Buford Brown, who was a colorful character on the waterfront. He had been a sailor associated with the Sailors' Union of the Pacific and was now operating as a pimp. Stormy Jean was both his wife and employee. Her specialty was "rolling" her customers—she would take payment first without rendering services afterward. Anderson told Detective Walter Graven that there was a police warrant out for her after she "rolled a man for $600." Evidently, she had not shared a cut with the officers.

Years later, in 1952, when Earl Anderson learned that the Multnomah Sheriff's Office was investigating connections between the Podlas and Schultze murders, he encouraged Graven to listen to the recorded conversation between Utah and Turman.

Answering Utah's question about why Jo Ann Dewey was killed, Turman explained that "she said, 'Buford killed Podlas—he's in the water,'" at which point both brothers start to laugh. In his personal notebook, Graven notes that the reason they laugh is that Dewey apparently got the story wrong. Schultze, not Podlas, had been put in the water and found in a shallow creek in North Portland not far from the Columbia River. This suggests that Buford killed Schultze. Elsewhere, Turman refers to Podlas's killing as a "copycat" murder, which is accurate given that both men were garroted. In another part of the recorded conversation, Turman says, "Ed said what I'm going to have to do is get rid of Jo Ann Dewy. She said, 'I know what's going on around here—Podlas murder. He's going to pay for it.'"

Graven went on to discover that the following people were involved in Podlas's murder in April 1948: Utah, the Duncans (including Jean), Neal Jacoby and Arthur Lombardi. In the recordings, Utah several times reassures Turman that "Neal and Arthur won't squawk" because they are in San Francisco. Graven and Anderson determined that both individuals were associated with the Sailors' Union of the Pacific and that Jacoby was known as a triggerman for the union. Graven

Walter Graven suffered hearing loss as a guard at the Kaiser shipyard during the war. As a Multnomah County deputy, he needed help from his wife and police officer son to decipher the recordings of the Wilson brothers' conversations. Photographer unknown. *Courtesy of the Walter Graven Estate.*

would later confirm that Jacoby was paid for the Podlas job and had driven a 1948 Dodge panel truck that witnesses saw parked at Third Avenue and West Burnside Street near Burke's Café, as well as on Germantown Road near the spot where Podlas's body was found. Graven would also discover that Stormy Jean Duncan was the last person seen with Podlas before he disappeared and turned up dead. She was, in fact, the mysterious blonde at whom newspapers hinted but apparently could not pursue.

The question for Graven and Anderson then became: "Why did Podlas and Schultze die and how were they connected?" The answer rests within an intricate web of organized crime, the likes of which Portland had not seen before. In fact, the web is so extensive that Graven and Anderson could not expose it at the time, which explains why every time attempts were made to apprehend the Duncans, they were tipped off and fled. As Graven would learn from Eddie Duncan's former girlfriend, Eleanor Sessions (who was hiding out in fear for her life at her parents' house on the Oregon coast),

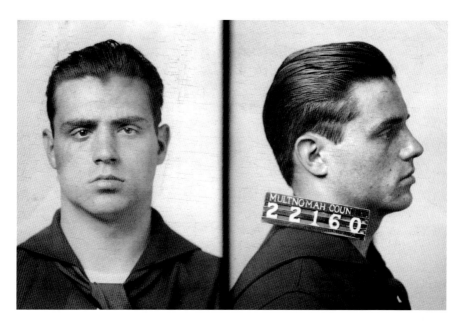

The Portland police believed that Neal Jacoby was a "trigger man for the Sailor's Union." He was in town at the time of the Podlas and Schultze killings, but possible connections to the Sailor's Union were not investigated until years later. Photographer unknown. *Courtesy of the Walter Graven Estate.*

"Dope [heroin] was behind it all." Among personal possessions left behind by Pierre Schultze at the YMCA where he had stayed were hypodermic needles and syringes along with forged papers identifying him as a detective for a steamship line. Graven would learn that he was attempting to blackmail a young man Graven identified as James B. Bradshaw III.

Moreover, another source close to Podlas informed authorities that the victim had been wearing a very expensive wristwatch that was missing when his body was found. The individual who tipped police off about this was James B. Bradshaw III, son of a wealthy Portland businessman. This aspect of the case, along with the discovery of the body in the wooded west hills of Portland, led authorities to draw initial parallels between Podlas's murder and the killing of Captain Frank Tatum the previous year. However, detectives pursuing the case several years later would learn that Bradshaw had misled police and that, in actuality, there had been no valuable wristwatch missing.

Research has not revealed a prominent Bradshaw family in Portland at the time. It has, however, revealed a Parker family, of which John J. Parker III was the wealthy successor. Newly discovered correspondence with

Washington state governor Arthur B. Langlie prior to the execution of the Wilson brothers reveals that Mrs. John J. Parker (who owned several movie theaters in Portland at the time) had a consort by the name of Jack Paris. In a letter to Langlie dated November 21, 1951, a yet unidentified writer described to the governor a particularly striking series of recent encounters with a young Portland woman named Muriel Hammond. Muriel had come into the care of the writer and several others after she stumbled into a North Portland church, where the writer was preaching. She was intoxicated and eventually confided in the writer that she was afraid to talk because she "would get what Jo Ann Dewey got." She explained that she had become pregnant and contacted her brother-in-law, J.J. Parker III, in Los Angeles. Parker arranged for his Portland associate (and mother's boyfriend) Jack Paris to take Muriel to Walla Walla, where an abortion was performed. On the way to Walla Walla, Jack Paris told her that "Jo Ann Dewey was a tramp and she got what was coming to her because she talked too much." He went on to explain, "They took her off the streets of Vancouver and took her to some brush and gave her the works." Muriel also told the writer that Parker had gotten her hooked on Benzedrine and other illicit drugs when he was in Portland. On several occasions, she contacted the writer, and he and his companions picked her up in a highly intoxicated state from a house behind the Surf Tavern near the intersection of Northeast Eighteenth and Alberta Avenues. In his personal notes, Graven mentions several times that the house behind the Surf Tavern was where the Duncans' sister Annie Sorensen lived, along with other women. She was often visited by well-known Portland sports concessions operator Paul Ail, who, Graven notes, "paid money when any [of the Duncans] got in trouble." In fact, he had paid Eddie's bail for deserting from the army back in 1947, shortening his jail time by half. At one point in Turman's recorded conversation to Utah, he exclaims, "I always knew he was a deserter!"

Near the end of her life, Jo Ann had told friends that she was afraid of a man named Johnny. This might have been Johnny Revisch, except that Jo Ann contacted him the night of the abduction and frequently got rides home from Portland with him. It might have been Stormy Jean's ex-husband, Buford Brown, who sometimes went by the nickname Johnny Kilbane (after a famous Cleveland boxer), but he seemed to have left town by the early 1950s. Most likely, it was Johnny Garrigues, a cousin of the Duncans who ran several taverns and restaurants in Portland and Vancouver. Nicknamed New York Johnnie, he was connected to Paul Ail.

This Johnnie ran the numbers on Thoroughbred horseracing in Vancouver and North Portland, and Ail ran concessions at the racetrack. In the early coverage of the Podlas murder, the *Oregonian* had specified that Podlas was interested in Thoroughbred racing and had discussed the subject with his former Vanport College math instructor, but this detail disappeared from subsequent stories about the case. There was also the fact that Podlas was trying to leave Portland because someone was after him. He had owed money previously, but the issue did not seem to be a lack of funds. A check for over $200 was found in his apartment after his murder. Rather, he was trying to shirk the people that he owed money to, and his plan was to get out of town on board a ship. The problem was that he was a member of the Sailors' Union of the Pacific, and the insiders there knew his game. Each of his efforts to sail was denied, and early in the week of April 6, 1948, the trap was set. Stormy Jean Duncan picked him up at Burke's Café, where he had been spending time, and he disappeared shortly thereafter. Podlas might have been present at Schultze's murder, or he might not have. The important fact was that he knew this gang, and like Schultze, he had tried to cross them.

Jo Ann Dewey, Roman Podlas and Pierre Schultze all tried to cross the Duncans and their gang, and each faced a rough end as a result. Not surprisingly, another parallel involved the law enforcement officials who pursued all three cases. When the investigation into connections between the Podlas and Schultze murders was ordered by Multnomah County sheriff Terry Schrunk in 1951, Portland police captain and Red Squad member William "Big Bill" Browne put his stepson Robert McKeown on the job, along with Floyd Smith, a detective specializing in extortion crimes. "Big Bill" himself had been the Portland police spokesperson to the press during the initial Podlas investigation. And it was "Big Bill," according to FBI files on the Dewey case, who told Vancouver police on March 27, 1950, to pick up the Wilson brothers as suspects in the case. Back in 1942, Portland police had arrested Wilson brothers Turman, Rassi and Glenn. Among other more serious charges, including rape, they had stolen over $2,000 in nickels from slot machines at taverns and clubs in the Portland area belonging to "Big Jim" Elkins. The arresting officer turned out to be Bard Purcell, brother of Captain (later Chief) "Diamond Jim" Purcell. During the McClellan vice hearings of the late 1950s, when the Jo Ann Dewey case and the Wilson brothers were a fading memory, Robert Kennedy and his team would reveal the close connections between "Diamond Jim" Purcell and "Big Jim" Elkins.

Walter Graven had been optimistic about closing the Podlas case, but by the time this picture was taken with his fellow deputies in 1952, he was convinced that "someone doesn't want me to solve this case." Photographer unknown. *Courtesy of the Walter Graven Estate.*

As the stories of Schultze, Podlas and Dewey reveal, the lawmakers from Washington were evidently concerned with a lot more than bootlegging, pinball and gambling, but even the United States government could not expose the real story at that point.

In the midst of their efforts to connect the Schultze, Podlas and Dewey cases, a news story broke that provided Graven and Anderson with additional details about key figures allegedly involved. On Monday, August 18, 1952, three men had been arrested and charged with badly beating up a sailor named Harold Kyle aboard the SS *Augustine Daly*, recently put into port after returning from Asia. William Benz, port agent for the Sailors' Union of the Pacific, and union members Luke A. Terry and George Bombareto were arrested. Benz told detectives and the press that the "fight" broke out when he and two union men questioned Kyle about "trouble on the trip." Benz claimed that Kyle went on to attack another sailor identified only as "the bos'n" in a nearby tavern and bit off the end of the man's finger in the scuffle. Benz described Kyle as "a trouble maker who has been kicked out of every maritime union in the country for past fights at sea."

In the ensuing trial several weeks later, Kyle told a different story, explaining that he was severely beaten by six men in his cabin aboard the *Augustine Daly* after an argument concerning dues to the union. While Benz testified that Kyle simply received the "worst end of a fight," Kyle insisted that he was helpless as the six men beat him mercilessly, severely wounding him in the head and face. The court sided with Kyle, sentencing Benz and Bombareto to thirty days in jail and issuing a fine of $100 to each man. The third man, Luke A. Terry, was freed because he could not be positively identified. Later, Kyle would disclose to Walter Graven that among the others involved who were not arrested was Arthur Lombardi. Graven would also learn that Roman Podlas had had several run-ins with William Benz at the Sailors' Union prior to his 1948 abduction and murder.

On September 2, 1952, Walter Graven wrote a letter to Sheriff Schrunk. In a previous correspondence with the sheriff, he had been optimistic about the prospects of solving the Schultze and Podlas cases, but now the tone was different. Citing ill health along with other factors, Graven asked to be relieved of his assignment to these cases. He explained that Schrunk himself had asked Graven and his partner Jack Wills to look into the recordings and to investigate possible connections between the murders. Yet at every turn, Graven faced resistance. His own boss, chief criminal detective Holger Christoffersen, refused to help out and ignored the dozen case reports that Graven and Wills attempted to file when the case was reopened in 1952. As Graven went on to explain to Schrunk:

> *I wish also to state that my investigations and findings have been made available to City Detectives, but at no time have I been informed as to what information they have, and I feel that cooperation should work both ways. I also cannot help but wonder why all information on the case has been kept from our own Department, but has been made readily available to the whole City Department.*

Graven went on to advise Schrunk that Utah Wilson, the Duncans and others were involved in the murders of Pierre Schultze and Roman Podlas and that Larry and Eddie Duncan abducted Jo Ann Dewey even though the Wilsons (at least Turman) were involved as well. Ending on a hopeful note, Graven expressed, "If my stepping aside so that someone else can finish this case will help bring these murderers to justice, then I readily do so, for, regardless of who does it, it should be done." Despite the optimism, as well as continuing efforts by Earl Anderson into the mid-1950s, these cases were never solved and all but faded from memory.

11

ROLLA CRICK AND THE ABORTIONISTS

You know the type of business we do. It is all over the grapevine. And the irony of it all is that we do [abortions for] *policemen and courthouse wives and the district attorney's office.*
—Johanna Eizema

Around the time that a jury was deciding that the Wilson brothers would hang, another Dewey unrelated to Jo Ann was facing scrutiny at his Portland chiropractic practice. Sometime in June 1950, two city police detectives had infiltrated the clinic while Dr. H.R. Dewey was in the process of a "clean-up" abortion job. His patient, an unnamed prostitute, had tried to end the pregnancy herself, and now the doctor was helping to complete the procedure. The two detectives confronted Dewey and allegedly told him to pony up $10,000 or they would send the case to district attorney John B. McCourt for prosecution. Dewey replied with a curt, "Go fly a kite." The detectives countered by requesting $5,000, and this was also refused. After the detectives left, they apparently stayed true to their promise and submitted the case to the district attorney.

Just over a year later and coinciding with a series of news stories in the *Oregon Journal* by Rolla "Bud" Crick, Portland police, accompanied by journalists from both the *Journal* and the *Oregonian*, conducted the largest citywide raid on abortion clinics in Portland history. Twelve people were arrested in the first round on July 6, 1951, including Dr. George H. Buck, Dr. Ross Hills Elliot, Dr. H.G. Weigar, Dr. E.V. Brandt and Dr. Kenneth Dewey (son of H.R. Dewey). Several days later, police officers booked

Rolla "Bud" Crick was an investigative reporter for the *Oregon Journal* who was dedicated to exposing Jim Elkins's operation. Photographer unknown. *Courtesy of the Portland Police Historical Society.*

Dr. H.R. Dewey, his nurse Doris Hofstra and Dr. Ruth Barnett. All were charged with "manslaughter by abortion" and "operation of a nuisance," which was the legal parlance for running an abortion "mill."

Among those rounded up in the raid, Ruth Barnett of the Stewart Clinic was arguably the most familiar to Portland newspaper readers. In 1940, Barnett had appeared in the Portland papers following the raid of a Reno, Nevada abortion clinic where she had been assisting. She had also appeared in the papers after falling victim to four robberies at her home in Portland throughout the 1940s. In one case, thieves hauled away a safe containing $50,000, at the time the "largest cash loot in Portland police annals." According to Barnett, $10,000 belonged to her, and the remaining $40,000 was the property of her pinball operator husband, Earl Bush (though later Bush would state that only $5,000 total was in the safe). By the time she was arrested in July 1951, Barnett's naturopathic practice was well established as "the city's most elaborate abortion parlor." Operating on the eighth floor of the posh Broadway building downtown (the site of Nordstrom today), the Stewart Clinic provided countless abortions per year to women rich and poor alike. Patients ranged from a young woman sexually assaulted by her first cousin to a suave "John" who unflinchingly brought over a dozen young prostitutes into the practice over the stretch of a few months.

Barnett had started her career as a dental assistant and then worked for Dr. Alys Griff, Portland's premier female physician in the early twentieth century. Among other services, Griff performed abortions, and Barnett learned the procedures from her. Barnett herself had had an abortion at the age of sixteen when a boyfriend had abandoned her after learning that she was pregnant. As she described it in her 1969 autobiography, *They Weep on My Doorstep*, "I was relieved of an exaggerated burden of apprehension and terror that inevitably comes to a young, unmarried girl." In the 1930s, Barnett began to work for Dr. George Watts in the Broadway building and eventually bought the practice from his successors. At that point, she had earned a naturopathic license, and her business flourished. Reflecting on her career in 1969, Barnett estimated that she had performed over forty thousand abortions and that she had earned nearly $2 million in her practice. She also made clear that she performed abortions only when danger was posed to the mother and that she turned many pregnant women away, having given the expectant mothers layettes and making them promise to raise their babies instead of seeking abortions elsewhere. As her nurses and assistants would attest, the procedure rooms were highly sterilized and fitted with modern medical equipment. The waiting rooms and offices were also lavishly appointed with dark furniture and oriental rugs, reflecting Barnett's personal taste. After each procedure, patients were sent to the similarly well-appointed Ramona Court Motel on Southwest Barbur Boulevard for rest and recovery. Such facilities stood in stark contrast to the often dangerous and unsanitary conditions facing abortion patients in the wake of the police crackdowns.

While awaiting trial with the others indicted in 1951, Barnett made headlines again on August 31, when two Portland police detectives were snared by a grand jury and accused of offering Dr. Barnett a $10,000 bribe. Detectives William L. Brian and O. Michael O'Leary surrendered to the charges. Shortly afterward, it was revealed that the same two detectives had also solicited a bribe from Dr. Dewey around the same time. Their attorney, Larry Landgraver, called foul, stating, "It's absolutely ridiculous that the same grand jury that voted to indict Barnett—and Dewey—would turn around and vote indictments against two policemen on the testimony of people the grand jury accused of being abortionists." Barnett and the other practitioners would eventually go on to face guilty verdicts, and many, including Barnett, would close their clinics and serve periodic jail time. Brian and O'Leary, however, were acquitted of the extortion charges on lack of evidence despite Barnett's precise description of the incident on the witness stand. She explained that she had withdrawn $4,000 from her office safe and another $6,000 from her deposit box at the First National Bank and then proceeded to meet Detective Brian at the corner of West Burnside Street and West Twentieth Avenue. At that point, she explained, she got into the passenger seat of his civilian car, and when they had parked at a secluded spot on Southwest Vista Drive off of Burnside Street, she handed him the money.

Barnett's sentencing (including several jail terms at the Rocky Butte Jail and at the Oregon State Penitentiary) and the acquittal of the detectives ushered in a new dawn for abortion providers in Portland. District attorney John B. McCourt's success in prosecuting abortionists on charges of "maintaining a public nuisance" set a powerful precedent that would ensure that abortion services would now have to go underground or out of town. At the same time, despite the vice crackdown initiated by William Lambert and Wallace Turner's *Oregonian* coverage and pursued by the McClellan hearings of 1956–57, prostitution continued to flourish in the Rose City. With it came a continuing demand for the services that providers like Barnett had offered. Although Barnett and some of her associates continued to perform abortions through the 1950s and into the 1960s (and also continued to face jail time for doing so), many Portlanders seeking these procedures found themselves looking beyond the city to destinations such as The Dalles and neighboring Dallesport, Washington. In the wake of the vice probe, many houses of prostitution and other illicit establishments relocated to those areas as well.

When *Oregon Journal* reporter Rolla J. "Bud" Crick started down the path of exposing the alleged "abortion racket" in Portland in the early 1950s, there is startling evidence that his primary goal was to shed light on civic corruption and the infiltration of organized crime into city government rather than simply to put an end to abortions. In Crick's recently discovered personal notebook from the period, he meticulously recorded the names of prostitutes and their associates, including information about police pay-offs. Among these was the testimony of several prostitutes and madams. Here is what he notes about Goldie Lewis, a forty-four-year-old madam:

> [She is] *threatening to tell how much, who, and why she pays off. She's sore because she can't run* [operate brothels] *and others do. She has been in the basement at 3237 NE Rodney but it's closed too. Her place is known as "The Door." She says she pays no policemen directly, but if she doesn't pay, police cars park in front of her place and she has to close.*

Nearly a dozen *Oregonian* articles from the period 1949 to 1954 confirm that Goldie Lewis was arrested at least nine times on the "morals charge" of "bringing two together for immoral purposes" at 3237 Northeast Rodney Street. Evidently, she was not cooperating with the pay-offs.

Left: Detective O. Michael O'Leary was accused of soliciting bribes and was on the payroll of "Concessions King" Paul Ail. Photographer unknown. *Courtesy of the Portland City Archive 2014-044.*

Right: Portland detective William L. Brian, O'Leary's partner, also provided vital information to Washington authorities involved in prosecuting the Wilson brothers. Brian was also accused of soliciting bribes. Photographer unknown. *Courtesy of the Portland City Archive A2014-004.*

Among other statements by prostitutes working across Oregon and Washington, Crick records the following information:

> *Two call girls, early in 1953, implicated* [Portland police detective Robert] *McKeown,* [William] *Brian, and* [Michael] *O'Leary in pay-offs. One said McKeown came to her apartment and suggested if she wanted to run he understood the price was $500.00 for a telephone* [i.e. to have a phone directory listing]. *She only knew O'Leary as his partner. The other girl (Shirley?) said Brian told her he understood houses were paying $250.00 per girl to run.*

Brian and O'Leary were the same detective partners accused of attempting to bribe abortion providers who happened to be treating prostitutes several years earlier. Revelations about their bribe efforts coincided with the abortion clinic raids and the appearance of Rolla Crick's *Oregon Journal* articles exposing the "abortion racket" in early July 1951. Bob McKeown, it should be recalled, was one of the Portland detectives (along with Floyd Smith) charged with investigating the Podlas and Schultze murders when Sheriff Schrunk ordered a new probe in 1951. McKeown and Smith had been assigned to the case by McKeown's stepfather, chief of detectives William "Big Bill" Browne (himself the original spokesman to the press on the Podlas case). On another page of the notebook, Crick notes that on December 29, 1953, Portland district attorney John B. McCourt's life was "threatened by a bomb supposed to be attached to his car by George Bernard for $500.00. Bob McKeown tipped by Bernard." A few pages later, Crick notes, "Bernard wanted rubber gloves from Jim Elkins at time of McCourt bomb plot. Said he had dynamite for years and grenades buried at the beach."

In the personnel files of Michael O'Leary and William Brian at the Portland City Archives are several striking documents. The first is a letter written to the chief of Portland police Charles Pray, dated July 13, 1950, by Clark County prosecuting attorney R. DeWitt Jones. It is worth quoting in full.

> *Dear Chief Pray:*
>
> *It has been my intention to call on you personally and express to you my sincere appreciation for the wonderful assistance and fine cooperation which I received from men in your department in connection with the investigation and trial of the Jo Ann Dewey case. Several persons in your department gave us valuable assistance, and I was particularly grateful for the help received from Mike O'Leary and William Brian of the Detectives Department. They uncovered some valuable evidence in the early days of the investigation and during the trial were most helpful in checking certain persons in Portland who were testifying for the defendants in connection with their alibi. Altogether we had exceptional cooperation for which I am personally appreciative. As Prosecutor of Clark County, I extend sincere thanks for the residents of Clark County.*
>
> *During the years I have been in my present work, I more and more realize the importance of having competent men, adequately paid, performing the field work in connection with the enforcement of our laws. I have constantly talked for and urged better compensation for men in this field. It is my firm belief that police work should be considered in the category of a profession and that requirements for this work should be high with a corresponding salary consistent with the qualification requirements. I believe that more money spent at this level would result in substantial saving to the public by a better protection of property and person.*

I would be glad to have you extend my thanks as expressed herein to the Mayor and Commissioners of your city. If at any time I may reciprocate in some small way to you, your department, and the City of Portland, please feel free to call upon me.

Sincerely yours,
DeWitt Jones, Prosecuting Attorney.

The second item is a stack of official police forms in Michael O'Leary's personnel file. The forms make clear that between about 1950 and 1970 (around the time that he retired from the force), O'Leary held additional jobs in the capacity of "seller" at Portland Meadows horse racing track, the Multnomah Kennel Club dog racetrack and the state fair in Salem. His employer in each case was Paul Ail Concessions, the same Paul Ail who had paid money whenever the Duncan family and their associates got into trouble—the same Duncans whom Earl Anderson and Walter Graven confirmed were at the heart of the Podlas, Schultze and Dewey murders.

A TRUTH THAT WILL SHOCK YOU

Do you know that in the world of the insane you will find a kind of truth more terrifying than fiction, a truth that will shock you? This is my world...let me lead you into it...nightmares of the daughter of horror are real.
—Daughter of Horror *(1955)*

Turman and Utah Wilson were hanged at the Washington State Penitentiary in January 1953. Their deaths closed the book on the Jo Ann Dewey case, providing a false sense of closure for the young woman's family. The cover up of the Podlas and Schultze murders held, and those crimes faded from public memory. By that time, Dorothy McCullough Lee's reform movement had spluttered and died. She lost her bid for reelection in 1952. Fred Peterson, city council member and former pharmacist, took over as mayor in 1953 and reinstated government by and for the "good-old-boys." It was back to business as usual in Portland, except Al Winter moved to Las Vegas to open the Sahara Hotel and strengthen his ties to the underworld. Jim Elkins was in charge now, and with his handpicked police chief—Jim Purcell—in office, he did things his way. That is, until the Teamsters' Union challenged him for power, touching off the vice scandal in 1956.

The exposure of the vice scandal and the McClellan hearings brought unwanted, embarrassing publicity to Portland. In the spring of 1957, before the hearings were complete and while the grand jury was still deciding on indictments, Allied Artists motion pictures sent a crew to Portland to make a quickie film on the scandal called *Portland Exposé*. The low-budget

THE WILSON BROTHERS: THE VERDICT WAS "GUILTY"

The execution of the Wilson brothers brought a false sense of closure for Jo Ann Dewey's family. It would take more than a generation for the story to start coming out that they had not been alone in the plot against Dewey. Photographer unknown. *Courtesy of the Earl Anderson Estate.*

potboiler was shot in Portland in a couple of weeks in May and June and was ready for release in August. It was shown once in Portland, at a screening for Mayor Terry Schrunk, Walter Langley, William Lambert, Wallace Turner and members of the city's Motion Picture Board of Censors. Although there was little to object to—other than the script, acting and production values—the film's premiere, scheduled simultaneously in Portland and Seattle, was canceled. Producer Lindsley Parsons blamed the cancelation on "pressure from interested parties" and then promptly issued posters for the film emblazoned, "Now Banned in Portland."

In September, the film opened in Washington, D.C.; Chicago; and a few other large markets. But within a week, its run had ended, and the film sank into obscurity. *Portland Exposé* was not seen in Portland until a three-day run at the Northwest Film Center in 1983, and it was released on DVD after Phil Stanford's *Portland Confidential* came out twenty years later. *Portland Exposé* made a strong point that Portland had been cleaned up and was now a "good clean place in which to live," but that theory only held if you forgot the stories of the Duncan, Wilson and Dewey families. The picture hinted at the violence that the McClellan committee ignored but did nothing to stir up memories of the forgotten crimes that haunted Portland.

Another film, by a Portland filmmaker but shot in Los Angeles, attempted to deal with the guilt and horror that lingered under the surface of the city's history. In 1955, this little-known film saw its United States premiere at the Fifty-fifth Street Playhouse in New York City. Titled *Dementia* when it was first made in 1953, American censors found the preliminary version distasteful for audiences and insisted that changes be made. The revised film would later be called *Daughter of Horror*, and it featured several cut scenes as well as narration to accompany the dialogue-free production.

The film follows a young woman (referred to in the credits as the Gamin) on a nightmarish late night journey through skid row. She encounters an array of rough characters, including a wife-abuser, a pimp, jazz musicians, heroin addicts and a portly rich man who tries to take advantage of her but falls prey to her switchblade. Although largely forgotten, the film has been heralded in recent years as an exemplary work of mid-twentieth-century expressionist noir in the tradition of Robert Wiene's 1920 masterpiece, *The Cabinet of Dr. Caligari*. Less attention, though, has been paid to its similarly forgotten creator, John J. Parker III. Although actor Bruno Vesota made clear in interviews that he played a role in the production of the film (in addition to playing the rich man), Parker was the uncredited writer, producer and director. Despite efforts to set up his own movie studio, Parker fell on difficult financial times as a result of squandering his fortune. He tried unsuccessfully to sue for control of his inheritance (a trust managed by his mother, Mrs. J.J. Parker), and he died in 1981. As it would turn out, Parker's single feature film would stand as his legacy.

Much lore surrounds the genesis of the film. The accompanying notes in a recent DVD release suggest that Parker came to the idea after learning about a dream that his assistant, Adrienne Barrett, had had about a horrific night on skid row. Parker was supposedly so struck by her account that he made the film and put her in the starring role as the Gamin. However, the film's voice-overs and narrative arc, coupled with the revelations about Parker's business dealings discussed in previous chapters, suggest a different explanation. In this light, the film becomes a kind of abstract confession whereby the Gamin's encounters intertwine with Parker's own experiences and associates, including Jo Ann Dewey herself.

Startling parallels to real life permeate the film, from the wave of water that overtakes the Gamin in her opening dream to the bushy-haired man booked for spousal abuse and led away by officers in the seedy hotel to the Gamin's descent into prostitution and downfall at the hands of pimps and fat cats. By killing the rich man who attempts to prostitute her, the Gamin asserts her own self-agency in a way that parallels Jo Ann Dewey's efforts to expose those who sought to control her. As the Gamin runs down the grand staircase of the lavish hotel, a finely dressed older woman makes her way up, ostensibly to see the rich man whom the Gamin has just killed. The older woman's clothing and appearance are a dead ringer for Mrs. J.J. Parker. Even a flower girl who lurks ominously in several scenes on the streets of skid row parallels a real figure. Ada Rathkey, "The Flower Girl of Portland," wrote a letter to Washington state governor Langlie in 1951 explaining how she herself was nearly abducted by the Duncan gang in North Portland. She, like many people who survived on the streets of Portland, was very aware of the threat the gang posed.

As the Gamin's journey spirals increasingly toward terror and destruction, the narrator (played by Ed MacMahon) chimes in ominously:

> *The hammer of the neon lights...forcing you to remember your guilt...forcing you to go back into the terror you are trying to forget...back through the mists of time into the graveyard where your secrets lie buried from the world.*

At the end, after the Gamin has killed the rich man, taken shelter among drug users and jazz aficionados and run from corrupt policemen back to the safety of her hotel room, the narrator's voice returns:

> *Only a dream...a dream of madness on a dark night...or was it? Was it only a dream?*

Parker's feelings of guilt and the "dream" that he used to cover them up are only now being recognized by Portlanders, more than sixty years later. The city is finally waking up from the nightmare of its history.

BIBLIOGRAPHY

Note: One of the main sources of this work is contemporary daily newspapers, such as the *Oregon Journal* and the *Oregonian*, available through the Multnomah County Library. Full subject indexes of articles used are available, but it would take too much space to publish them here.

Abbott, Carl. "From Urban Frontier to Metropolitan Region: Oregon's Cities from 1870–2008." *Oregon Historical Quarterly* 110, no. 1 (Spring 2009): 74–95.

Anderson, Earl. Unpublished Papers, Letters and Investigation Notes. Earl Anderson Estate. Courtesy of Matthew Anderson.

Baker, Doug, and Ruth Barnett. *They Weep on My Doorstep*. Beaverton, OR: Halo, 1969.

Barbash, Jack. "The Labor Movement after World War II." *Monthly Labor Review* 99, no. 11 (November 1976): 34–37.

Bennett, Charles. "Legendary Lawman August Vollmer." *Officer.com*. http://www.officer.com/article/10232661/legendary-lawman-august-vollmer.

Bigelow, William. "Agitate, Educate, Organize: Portland 1934." *Oregon Historical Quarterly* 89, no. 1 (Spring 1988): 4–29.

Bonthius, Andrew. "Origins of the International Longshoremen's and Warehousemen's Union." *Southern California Quarterly* 59, no. 4 (Winter 1977): 379–426.

Brodey, Jesse W. "Racketeering: An American Institution." *Social Science* 12, no. 1 (January 1937): 46–53.

BIBLIOGRAPHY

Carter, Joan Mae. *Unjust Treatment: The True Story of Jo Ann Dewey and the Wilson Brothers*. Olympia, WA: privately published, n.d.

Carter, Sandy. "Oregon Voices: Letters From Bob: A GI Re-Entering Portland Life in 1945." *Oregon Historical Quarterly* 106, no. 4 (Winter 2005): 616–41.

City Club of Portland. "Law Enforcement in Portland and Multnomah County." *Portland City Club Bulletin*.

———. The Negro in Portland, 1945." *Center for Columbia River History*. http://www.ccrh.org/comm/slough/primary/1945rpt.htm.

Crick, Rolla. *Reporter's Notebook*. Portland Police Historical Society. Unpublished, 1950–1953.

Dietsche, Robert. *Jumptown: The Golden Years of Portland Jazz, 1942–1957*. Corvallis: Oregon State University Press, 2005.

Donnelly, Robert C. *Dark Rose: Organized Crime and Corruption in Portland*. Seattle: University of Washington Press, 2011.

———. "Organizing Portland: Organized Crime, Municipal Government, and the Teamsters Union." *Oregon Historical Quarterly* 104, no. 3 (Fall 2003): 334–365.

DuPay, Don. "Behind the Badge in River City." Manuscript, 2012.

Fingard, Judith. "The Decline of the Sailor as a Ship Labourer in 19th Century Timber Ports." *Labour/Le Travail* 2 (1977): 35–53.

Fowler, Josephine. "New Approaches to Labor History: East to West and West to East: Ties of Solidarity in the Pan-Pacific Revolutionary Trade Union Movement, 1923–1934. *International Labor and Working Class History* 66 (Fall 2004): 99–117.

Gitelman, H.M. "Perspectives on American Industrial Violence." *Business History Review* 47, no. 1 (Spring 1973): 1–23.

Graven, Walter. *Unpublished Papers, Letters and Investigation Notes*. Walter Graven Estate. Courtesy of Gloria Graven.

Haller, Mark H., and John V. Alviti. "Loansharking in American Cities: Historical Analysis of a Marginal Enterprise." *American Journal of Legal History* 21, no. 2 (April 1977): 125–156.

Hanson, Howard. Interview with the authors, May 25, 2014.

Heustis, Carl E. "Police Unions." *The Journal of Criminal Law, Criminology, and Police Science* 48, no. 6 (March/April 1958): 643–46.

Hoffman, Dennis E., and Vincent J. Webb. "Police Response to Labor Radicalism in Portland and Seattle, 1913–1919." *Oregon Historical Quarterly* 87, no. 4 (Winter 1986): 341–66.

Jacobs, James B., and Ellen Peters. "Labor Racketeering: The Mafia and Unions." *Crime and Justice* 30 (2003): 229–82.

BIBLIOGRAPHY

Juris, Hervey A. "The Implications of Police Unionism." Special police issue, *Law & Society Review* 6, no. 2 (November 1971): 231–46.

Kennedy, Robert. *The Enemy Within*. New York: Harper, 1960.

King, Harry. *Box Man: A Professional Thief's Journey*. Edited by Bill Chambliss. New York: Harper & Row Publishers, 1972.

Langlie, Arthur. *Governor Langlie's Papers*. Olympia: Washington State Archive, n.d.

Lansing, Jewel. *Portland: People, Politics and Power, 1851–2001*. Corvallis: Oregon State University Press, 2003.

MacColl, E. Kimbark. *The Growth of a City: Power and Politics in Portland, Oregon 1915 to 1950*. Portland, OR: Georgian Press, 1979.

Marks, Monique, and Jenny Fleming. "The Right to Unionize, the Right to Bargain, and the Right to Democratic Policing." Special issue, *Annals of the American Academy of Political and Social Science* 605 (May 2006): 178–99.

Marsh, Floyd R. *20 Years a Soldier of Fortune*. Portland, OR: Binford and Mort, 1976.

Mazza, Dave. "Stanford Tale Leaves Readers Wanting More." *Portland Alliance*. February 8, 2005. http://www.theportlandalliance.org/2005/feb/portlandconfidential.htm.

McClary, Daryl C. "Turman G. Wilson and Utah E. Wilson Kidnap Jo Ann Dewey in Vancouver, Washington, on March 19, 1950." *HistoryLink. org*. 2010. http://www.historylink.org/index.cfm?DisplayPage=output. cfm&file_id=9573.

McLaglen, Elizabeth. *A Peculiar Paradise: A History of Blacks in Oregon, 1788–1940*. Portland, OR: Georgian Press, 1980.

Monkkonen, Eric H. "History of Urban Police." Special issue, *Crime and Justice* 15 (1992): 547–80.

Munk, Michael. *Portland Red Guide*. 2nd ed. Portland, OR: Ooligan Press, 2011.

———. "Portland's Radical Past." *Portland Alliance*, June 2000–August 2001. http://college.lclark.edu/programs/political_economy/student_resources/past.

———. "Portland's 'Silk Stockings Mob': The Citizens Emergency League in the 1934 Maritime Strike." *Pacific Northwest Quarterly* 91, no. 3 (Summer 2000): 150–60.

Murrell, Gary. "Hunting Reds in Oregon, 1935–1939." *Oregon Historical Quarterly* 100, no. 4 (Winter 1999): 374–401.

Nelson, Bruce. "Unions and the Popular Front: The West Coast Waterfront in the 1930s." Special issue, *International Labor and Working Class History* 30, (Fall 1986): 59–78.

Niete, Warren. "Enforcing Oregon's State Alcohol Monopoly: Recollections from the 1950s." *Oregon Historical Quarterly* 115, no. 1 (Spring 2014): 90–105.

BIBLIOGRAPHY

Oregon State Archive. "A Matter of Color: African Americans Face Discrimination." *Life on the Homefront: Oregon Responds to World War II.* http://arcweb.sos.state.or.us/pages/exhibits/ww2/life/minority.htm.

Palmateer, Dmitri. "Charity and the Tramp: Itinerancy, Unemployment, and Municipal Government from Coxey to the Unemployed League." *Oregon Historical Society* 107, no. 2 (Summer 2006): 228–53.

Pilcher, William W. *The Portland Longshoremen: A Dispersed Urban Community.* New York: Holt, Rinehart & Winston, 1972.

Pitzer, Paul C. "Dorothy McCullough Lee: The Successes and Failures of 'Dottie-Do-Good.'" *Oregon Historical Quarterly* 91, no. 1 (Spring 1990): 4–42.

Polishuk, Sandy, and Julia Ruutila. *Sticking to the Union: An Oral History of the Life and Times of Julia Ruutila.* New York: Palgrave McMillan, 2003.

Portland Police Bureau. *Personnel Files.* Portland City Archive.

Reiss, Albert J., Jr. "Police Organizing in the Twentieth Century." Special issue, *Crime and Justice* 15 (1992): 51–97.

Saposs, David J. "Labor Racketeering: Evolution and Solutions." *Social Research* 25, no. 3 (Autumn 1958): 253–70.

Schwartz, Stephen. *Brotherhood of the Sea: A History of the Sailors' Union of the Pacific.* Transaction Books. Oxford, UK: Rutgers University and Oxford, 1986.

———. "A History of the Portland Police Association, Local 456." *The PPA Rap Sheet.* May 3, 2013. http://pparapsheet.org/a-history-of-the-portland-police-association-local-456-2.

Springer, Frank. "Stories by Frank Kenneth Springer Sr." Manuscript, 2008.

Stanford, Phil. *Portland Confidential.* Portland, OR: Westwinds Press, 2004.

Stoops, Collie, and W.T. Taylor. Frank Tatum Murder Investigation File. Portland Police Historical Society, Portland, OR. Unpublished, 1947.

Taylor, Paul S. "Organization and Policies of the Sailors' Union of the Pacific." *Monthly Labor Review* 16, no. 4 (April 1923): 11–20.

Thorton, Robert Y. "Organized Crime in the Field of Prostitution." *Journal of Criminal Law, Criminology and Police Science* 775 (1955–1956): 775–79.

Witwer, David. "The Racketeer Menace and Antiunionism in the Mid-Twentieth Century US." *International Labor and Working Class History* 74 (Fall 2008): 124–47.

INDEX

INDEX

INDEX

ABOUT THE AUTHORS

J B Fisher teaches writing at Portland Community College. He came to the field of Portland crime history when he inadvertently discovered hidden above his water heater a stack of old *Oregon Journal* newspapers about a long-forgotten Oregon mystery. Fisher holds a doctorate in Renaissance English literature and was a Shakespeare professor before returning to the City of Roses, where he is now researching and writing about some of Portland's most intriguing unsolved crime cases.

Photograph by JB Fisher.

ABOUT THE AUTHORS

JD Chandler, a former labor union activist, is a native Oregonian. He is the author of two previous books on Portland history: *Hidden History of Portland, Oregon* (2013) and *Murder and Mayhem in Portland, Oregon* (2013). He is also the author of two blogs concerned with the history of Portland: "The Slabtown Chronicle," www.portlandcrime.blogspot.com and "Weird Portland," www.weirdportland.blogspot.com.

Photograph by Shirley Obitz.